MEDIA, FEMINISM, CULTURAL STUDIES

Stepping Forward: Essays, Lectures and Interviews
by Wolfgang Iser

Wild Zones: Pornography, Art and Feminism
by Kelly Ives

Global Media Warning: Explorations of Radio, Television and the Press
by Oliver Whitehorne

Andrea Dworkin
by Jeremy Mark Robinson

Cixous, Irigaray, Kristeva: The Jouissance of French Feminism
by Kelly Ives

Sex in Art: Pornography and Pleasure in Painting and Sculpture
by Cassidy Hughes

*The Erotic Object: Sexuality in Sculpture
From Prehistory to the Present Day*
by Susan Quinnell

Women in Pop Music
by Helen Challis

Detonation Britain: Nuclear War in the UK
by Jeremy Mark Robinson

Julia Kristeva: Art, Love, Melancholy, Philosophy, Semiotics
by Kelly Ives

Luce Irigaray: Lips, Kissing, and the Politics of Sexual Difference
by Kelly Ives

Helene Cixous I Love You: The Jouissance of Writing
by Kelly Ives

*The Poetry of Cinema
by John Madden*

The Sacred Cinema of Andrei Tarkovsky
by Jeremy Mark Robinson

Disney Business, Disney Films, Disney Lands
Daniel Cerruti

Feminism and Shakespeare
by B.D. Barnacle

'Cosmo Woman'

'COSMO WOMAN'

The World of Women's Magazines

Oliver Whitehorne

Crescent Moon

CRESCENT MOON PUBLISHING
P.O. Box 393
Maidstone
Kent, ME14 5XU
United Kingdom

First published 1997. Second edition 2008. Fourth edition 2010.
© Oliver Whitehorne 1997, 2008, 2010.

Printed and bound in the U.S.A.
Set in Garamond Book 9 on 14pt.
Designed by Radiance Graphics.

British Library Cataloguing in Publication data

Whitehorne, Oliver
'Cosmo' Woman: The World of Women's Magazines
1. Women's periodicals - 20th century - History and criticism
2. Women's periodicals, English - 20th century - History and criticism
I. Title
302. 2'324'082

ISBN-13 9781861712851

Contents

ACKNOWLEDGEMENTS

Every effort has been made to contact copyright owners of the illustrations. No copyright infringement is intended. We welcome enquiries about any copyright issues for future editions of this book.

Picture credits:

National Magazine Company. IPC Media. Panini. EMAP. D.C. Thomson. Conde Nast. BBC Magazines. Hachette Filipacchi. EMAP Metro.

For my sisters

COSMOPOLITAN

September 1993

Big Growth Areas!
Fellatio on the upswing, male multiple orgasms and other SEX findings for you to chew over

What we love about men's bodies (Why aren't we fussier?)

THE INCREDIBLE SULK
Why is he so unsupportive when you're supporting him?

COSMO EXCLUSIVE!
Meet Sue Townsend, Ben Elton, Cynthia Heimel and Scott Turow at our great Book Day

WOMEN WHO EAT TOO MUCH
How it feels and why they do it

Tender is the first sight
What makes the famous fall in love?

Why the Equal Opportunities Commission is utterly useless

The world's most delicious lesbian on love, SEX and men

I
THE WONDERFUL WORLD OF 'WOMEN'S MAGAZINES'

I LIKE MAGAZINES. They are fun, silly, superficial, informative, educational, patronizing, sexy, mad, wasteful, sleazy, naïve, inept, messy, profoundly capitalist, dull, and fascistic. Millions of magazines are sold every month. *Millions. Each month.* It's pricey launching a magazine, and expensive to run one. But if you get it right, and if customers buy it, the potential is enormous.

What applies to *Cosmopolitan* magazine in this book also applies to most 'women's magazines', and most populist magazines. I haven't rewritten some parts of this book, which was published in the mid-1990s. A lot has changed in magazine publishing and popular culture since 1996, true, but also, not much has changed at all. There's reality TV, i-Pods, the internet, cell phones. But in fact, contemporary culture is even more conservative, more complacent and more smug now – at least in Europe and America.

A magazine is like a club, which must flatter its readers, making them think they belong and are welcome in the club.[1] Magazines can stand in for friends, for the reader alone at home. As Carol Sarler, editor of *Honey* in the 1980s put it, 'at best, a magazine functions like a good friendship. There's contact, there's communication *both* ways'.[2] Most magazines

1 Jane Reed, editor of *Woman's Own*, in Hughes-Hallett, 1982, 21
2 Sarler, *Honey*, September 1983

operate in similar ways, with similar strategies, needs, goals. They all need advertizing • committed, hard-working journalists and editors • a constant flow of ideas and input • and newly launched products (films, books, cosmetics, cars). The cover price does not fund magazines: the cover price would have to be doubled to break even, said *Cosmo*'s publisher in 1983 (J. Winship, 1987, 38). They all need to maintain and if possible expand their readership. Subscribers who pay up each year are cherished – not only by small print-run academic journals (*Diacritics, Yale French Studies, Women's Review, Artforum, Journal of the History of Ideas*) – but also by the big glossy magazines (*Vogue, Cosmo, Arena, GQ*). Of the 2,500 magazines published only 130 are 'women's magazines'.

Magazines are intermediaries between consumers and consumer-producers. Magazines produce and reproduce 'hierarchies of value in their fields',[3] they are continually sorting out what is meaningful or valuable and what is not, what is 'in', what is 'out', what is desired, what is loathed, what the reader must have. Magazines require that their readers be skilled consumers, able to decode a plethora of commodity ads often advertized as little bits of bodies each with their own range of products: eyes, mouths, hands, nails, hair, etc. Every aspect of the late capitalist world has its range of products to help maintain it: lawnmowers, CDs, cars, paintings, kettles, clothes. With even seemingly 'narrow' items, such as cars, there are a host of products and ads. In car magazines, there are ads for certain types of engine, or particular roof racks, or hub caps. In pornography magazines, there are ads for distinct categories of sexual identity: gay, bi, group, S/M, old-young, lesbian, role playing, etc. No aspect/ activity of life, it seems, is free of its own range of commodities and ads.

The most bizarre magazines in Britain are those that cater for oddball specialist (too often masculinist) pursuits. Not just the usual suspects of 'kinky' or 'perverse' sexual desires (rubber, S/M, leather, etc) but those founded on keeping pigeons, garden fence maintenance and collecting train numbers. The really unusual elements of any magazine is the reader's letters or classified ads section. Even the ardent scrutiny of copy and sub-editors

---

3 Todd Gitlin: "The new video technology: pluralism or banality?", *Democracy*, 4, 1981, 68

cannot eradicate every oddball contributor that appears on the classifieds page. Here the barriers between producers, magazine and readers are at their thinnest, as readers offer commodities to other readers. Here we see individuals addressing other individuals, in all their unadorned, banal, awkwardly-phrased glory. For this reason, the *Exchange and Mart*, a British magazine, is one the most entertaining reads in Blighty, for it is full of bizarre, inane, simplistic and insidious adverts for second-hand goods. You can buy replica guns:

> Blank firing replicas that load, fire and eject – just like the real thing… Browning Hi-Power Classic 8mm 12-shot auto, £99.95… Colt Peacemaker, 9mm, £42.50.

The cover of a 1955 copy of *She* offered 'fiction, TV, gossip, letters, films, records, books, beauty, homework, strip-story, fashion, furnishing, knitting, quizzes, patterns, cookery, readers' problems'. 'Women's magazines' didn't alter their list of contents that much in the forty years between 1955 and 1995.

American *Cosmopolitan* was (partly) launched by Helen Gurley Brown, author of the bestseller, *Sex and the Single Girl*. Brown created the *Cosmopolitan* woman: single, sexual, working, into self-improvement. Circulation of the old Hearst magazine was 600,000: after 7 years with Helen Gurley Brown's vision, it reached 1,500,000; by 1977, it had reached 2,500,000 (with a cover price of $1.50). The current editor is Kate White.

The circulation in 2009 was 2.9 million.

British *Cosmopolitan* was launched with one of the most successful magazine publicity campaigns ever. The concept of the British '*Cosmo* girl' was essentially the same as the American one in terms of interests (job, men, travel, body, sex, fashion, cosmetics, arts) but with a psycho-social slant that was attuned to a British viewpoint. The first issue (of 300,000), helped by Saatchi & Saatchi TV ads, sold out on the first day. The second issue, which featured the male nude, sold out 450,000 in two days (far outselling its competitors, *Flair, Honey, Nova* and *Vanity Fair*)

In the United States of America, the biggest selling magazines in 2009 were: *AARP* 22.6 million, *AARP Bulletin* 22.075 million, *TV Guide* 8.2m, *Reader's Diget* 10.1m, *Better Homes* 7.6m, *National Geographic* 5.4m, *Good Housekeeping* 4.6m, *Family Circle* 4.3m, *Ladies' Home Journal* 4.1m and *Woman's Day* 4.04m. The circulation of newspapers, meanwhile, was daily 34.4 million, with 40 million on Sundays.

Honey had pioneered many of the formats and issues that 'women's magazines' of the 1980s and 1990s employed. In the 1960s, *Honey*, like *Nova* and *She*, was part of the creation of the so-called 'New Woman'. *Honey* was politicized ('THIS ISSUE CONCERNS YOU... HOW TO GET INVOLVED' proclaimed a March. 1967 cover). Indeed, it was due to the political (feminist) stance of an editor (Carol Sarler) that reportedly got her fired from *Honey* in the 1980s. Sarler had introduced a more aggressive form of feminism into *Honey* in the 1980s, and it was this, apparently, not falling circulation, that led to her departure (J. Winship, 1987, 20).

The following section looks at some of the key publications among 'women's magazines' in the United Kingdom of the past 30-40 years. Some have ceased publication, but that doesn't affect the arguments in this study too much: all magazines are clones, and every magazine copies every other magazine. At many levels, magazines are interchangeable (certainly within each niche or genre or format).

The title *Cosmopolitan* does not refer to some city listings magazine (cosmopolitan, like metropolis, sounds like a magazine such as *City Limits*). *Cosmopolitan* is, rather, a National Magazine Company (London) publication (part of the Hearst Group in North America) aimed at women who are career-minded, fashion-conscious, and loving life.[4] *Cosmopolitan* sells 456,703 copies every month in the U.K. (1994 figures), and is read by 2,300,000 adults.

Cosmopolitan is a format that has been reproduced around the world: there are editions of *Cosmo* in 34 languages – in India, Romania, Greece,

---

4 This is from an ad for National Magazine Company: '[s]pend a month with National Magazines and *Cosmopolitan, Harper and Queens, Good House-keeping, She* and *Company* will put you in touch with 33% of all ABC 1 women. Independent, discriminating, intelligent *and above all affluent*. Britain's most desirable women.' [my italics] *Campaign*, 18 April 1980

Italy, France, Brazil, Germany, etc. There are other elements to the *Cosmo* empire: Cosmo TV • Cosmo Radio • a spin-off magazine aimed at younger readers, *CosmoGIRL*, which was published from 1999 to 2008 (in America) • and of course an online presence.

On the web (such as at cosmopolitan.co.uk or cosmopolitan.com), *Cosmo* reproduces its magazine, with sections such as: love and sex, men, fashion and style, beauty, your life, community and dating.

In 2009, *Cosmo*'s ABC circulation in the U.K. was 460,276. In the U.S.A. it was 2.9 million in 2009. This compares with: *Glamour* 2.39 million, *InStyle* 1.73m, *Self* 1.3m, *Vogue* 1.3m, *Lucky* 1.12m, *Elle* 1.1m and *Allure* 1.09m.

There are jokes and snide comments in the media about the 'Cosmopolitan woman', a particular kind of stereotype who inhabits the media landscape somewhere between *Woman's Hour* and *Smash Hits*, between *The Clothes Show* (BBC TV show and magazine) and *Spare Rib*. *Cosmopolitan*, though a newish magazine, has established a world of its own, and is a key mover in the 'women's magazine' market. *Cosmopolitan* is at the centre of 'women's magazines', placed in the 'General Interest' section in newsagents, beside populist magazines such as *TV Times, Radio Times* and *Woman's Realm* and merging into the 'glossy' 'women's magazines', such as *Marie Claire* and *Vogue*. *Cosmopolitan* includes 'glossy' fashion items, as found in the 'high class' fashion magazines (*Marie Claire, Elle,* and *Tatler*). *Cosmopolitan* has a very distinctive place within the 'women's magazine' market, a place largely marked out by its crusading style.

Cosmopolitan occupies a phase in growth somewhere between teenage and motherhood. It speaks to single, career-orientated women. It is the magazine bought after *Jackie* and *19* have been left behind. A female reader, living between the 1960s and today somewhere in the Western world, might begin reading *The Brownie* (for 7-10 year olds), then move onto *Look-In*. During teenage s/he might consume *Smash Hits, Jackie, Just Seventeen* and *Mizz.* Then, s/he, in late teens and early twenties, might buy *Company, 19* and *Cosmopolitan.* Later, she might read *Bella, Best, Me,*

House & Garden, Vogue, Woman, Gardens News, Good Housekeeping, Mother and Baby, and, maybe, one of the magazines aimed at 'older readers'.

The *Radio Times* is a model mass popular magazine. As the largest-selling popular magazine in Great Britain, the *Radio Times* offers a barometer of the magazine market, and is worth looking at for that reason. It is an extraordinarily bland magazine. Or, rather, the *Radio Times* simply makes obvious the banality of most magazines, certainly most populist magazines, magazines not aimed at a specialist audience. The *Radio Times* is the pinnacle of blandness. The preview section (equivalent to the 'news', 'what's on' and 'diary' pages of 'women's magazines') takes up the front 50 or so pages; then comes the week's film guide, then the listings. After this, two or three pages of readers' letters, a horoscope page, a crossword puzzle, a preview of next week's edition of the magazine, and the back page, as with the Sunday newspaper colour supplements, features the 'day in the life' of some media celebrity.

The format of the *Radio Times* is very much that of the Sunday colour supplement magazines and 'women's magazines'. The preview section divides broadcasting into genres – gardening, sport, natural history, drama – and these categories reflect genre-based organization in the press and in broadcasting. The *Radio Times*, then, is a media magazine, a publication that fuses TV, radio and the press. It is all about fusion, so that the consumption of TV, radio and the press appear as one thing in the *Radio Times*. The idea is that you have a copy of the *Radio Times* on the arm of your armchair as you consume the media. The preview pages of the magazine are constructed in short bursts of relatively detailless information, very generalized accounts of the programmes on offer in the week ahead. There is an emphasis on bright, jolly colour images, usually of people. The cover always features grinning stars, the colours chosen are always meant to evoke pleasure. The effect of reading the *Radio Times* is that desired by some editors of 'women's magazines': it's like settling down for a five minute coffee break. Helen Chappell, who wrote for *Company* in the

1980s, said readers see magazines 'quite deliberately as mental chocolate – give or take a few hard nuts'.[5] The prose style is chatty, gossipy, light. 'Serious' issues are mentioned only in passing, and in one or two more 'weighty' editorial items per week. On the whole, the *Radio Times* steers well clear of controversy. The uncomfortable nature of the real world is only alluded to: deeply held feelings about, say racism, are firmly edited out of any features and copy.

She (circ. 283,731) is the magazine most like *Cosmopolitan,* perhaps, though it is aimed at a slightly older readership. *She* has features that go beyond the world of *Cosmopolitan,* beyond the run-up to marriage; *She* moves into articles on being a young mother, on child rearing and growing pains. As with *Cosmo*, the staff of *She* is mainly female, and the articles are written by and for women. Like *Cosmo*, and all 'women's magazines', *She* has features on career, interiors, food, going out, holidays, adultery, sex, health, beauty, horoscopes, crosswords, etc. The cover of April, 1994's *She* announces that *She* is 'for women who juggle their lives'. Around the photo of a perfectly formed woman (white, scrubbed, made-up, white European, affluent) we find the usual selection of menu tasters: 'The diet to end all diets', 'Is your body good enough for you?', 'How my sex life took a turn for the better' and 'Don't worry, all mothers worry – and always will'. *She* is for the *Cosmo* woman growing into young motherhood, with all the usual regular articles and features as found in all 'women's magazines' (beauty, health, horoscopes, problem page, fashion, sexuality) but aimed at a slightly older audience. *She* is a bridge between 'women's magazines' such as *Cosmopolitan, 19* and *Elle* and the 'older', more 'staid' 'women's magazines' such as *Bella, Woman's Own, Woman's Journal* and *Take a Break*.

Company (circ. 176,150) was launched in 1978, aiming at ABC1 18-24 year-old women. It is a sister magazine to *Cosmopolitan,* produced by the same publishing company (National Magazines Ltd). *Company* is essentially the same magazine as *Cosmopolitan,* same but different, as with other 'women's magazines' (all magazines) are 'the same but different'. A glance at a copy of *Company* reveals the usual glossy articles – on Hollywood

5 Helen Chappell: "Big sister", *New Society*, 5 May 1983

celebs, on 'the joy of weekend relationships' ('exciting sex, more romance, fewer arguments'), on shopping, on fashion, and on 'trash TV'. ('Trash television' is the soaps, sit-coms and game shows that high-minded critics appear to despise. *Company*, however, asserts that 'in some strange way [TV] soaps improve your mental health'.)[6]

Beside 'positive' and light features are 'hard-hitting' journalistic pieces, such as "Boys For Sale", about 'rent boys' (male prostitutes: 'already he's earned £120 for two hand-jobs and a blowjob'),[7] and a piece on hospitals for the mentally ill, one of those extremely thorny issues that societies find it easier to sweep under the carpet than solve. According to the numbing *Company* article, '50% of women in mental hospitals been sexually assaulted'.[8]

Options (circ. 150,000) is fussier and more practical/ 'serious' than *Cosmopolitan*, and includes features on being a mother. It was launched by IPC in 1982, initially aimed at ABC1 women aged between 22 and 44 (the '*Options* woman' has 'a calculator in her handbag, a stereo in her car, a note recorder at her office', according to the publicity material [J. Winship, 1987, 37]). £1 million ($1.6m) was spent launching it, with a print order of 390,000.

Vogue (circ. 181,912) is in some ways the archetypal 'glossy' 'women's magazine', having always, it seems, concentrated on fashion and looking good. Magazines such as *Vogue* are influential and may be partly responsible for the emphasis in 'women's magazines' on fashion and looks. *Mizz* (circulation 140,000) is aimed at 'young (15-19) girls',[9] and is colourful, zestful and fashion-conscious. *19* (circ. 190,000) is aimed at slightly older young women (17-22), and, like the defunct *Honey*, is a young version of *Cosmopolitan,* while *New Woman* is practically a copy of *Cosmopolitan.*

Like *New Woman, Marie Claire* (circulation 222,267) is a self-conscious 'women's magazine', combining international *Vogue*-style fashion and *The Face* graphics with one or two 'hard news' style investigative pieces, giving

---

6 Leah Hardy: "I Want My Trash TV", *Company*, November 1994, 93
7 Mandie Appleyard: "Boys For Sale", *Company*, November 1994, 413
8 "Women in Mental Hospitals", *Company*, November 1994, 109
9 Barry Turner, ed: *The Writer's Handbook 1993*, Macmillan 1993, 264

it a more 'serious' edge than many other 'glossy' 'women's magazines'.

Elle (founded by part of Rupert Murdoch's empire in 1985, circ. 250,000) is very similar to the *Marie Claire* and *Vogue*, also concentrating on the 'top names' in contemporary 'high fashion' with features on sexuality, finance, health, etc. 'In true postmodernist fashion, *Elle* documents consumption as a metaphor for life: the only choice is to consume'.[10] The editor of *Elle* said that women readers were fed up with lengthy articles on orgasms with a bit of fashion thrown in (*à la Cosmopolitan* and *Company*). *Elle* went for much shorter features. It was, Joyce Hopkirk claimed, 'primarily a style magazine with words' (B. Braithwaite, 79).

The Tatler (circ. 49,124) makes gossip and 'personal profiles' prominent, especially about royalty or the sort of upper-class and aristocracy that frequents Ascot and opera and other highlights of 'the season'. *Harpers & Queen* (circ. 82,767) is similarly yuppie/ Sloane Rangerish, horsey, featuring pictures of royalty and aristocracy at various dinners and 'high class' outings. Both *Tatler* and *Harpers & Queen* contain features that are extensions of Sunday supplement colour magazines, and those spots in the tabloid Sundays that print collections of snapshots of the 'glitterati' in evening dress taken at celebrity parties. In "Jennifer's Diary" in *Harper's & Queen*, people are described by their social title, reinforcing notions of class and status. For example, people are defined as '*Mr* George Burnand', '*Miss* Lucinda Murray', '*Lord* Swaythling', '*Viscountess* Windsor' and '*Princess* Alexandra'. These titles are the captions to colour photographs of the hoi poloi, the nobs, the 'aristocrats', the 'haves', who go to functions, dinners, garden parties and the like. Naturally, one doesn't see a non-white face in these snap-shots of the 'great and the good'. No, these are society luvvics, clad in designer dresses and sober dinner jackets. At the same time, *Harpers & Queen* and *Tatler* also aim to be 'streetwise' (B. Turner, ib, 252).

The Lady (circ. 66,000) has a distinctly 'upper class' feel, but offers the usual 'women's magazine' fare: fashion, beauty, household, gardening, shopping, finance. It is one of the most 'traditional' of 'women's

10 Janet Lee, in L. Gamman, 171

magazines'.

If *Tatler, Harpers & Queen, The Lady* and others seem sycophantic in their personality profiles and puff pieces, they are far surpassed by the unashamedly gossip-based magazines *Hello!* and *OK!* and their clones. If you are royal or a celebrity, you have lurid prose dripping with sycophancy and ass-lick written about you. *Hello!* and *OK!* are un-ironic in their ridiculous hype of the cult of personalities, but at least they do it with no holds barred. Nothing is held back in their adulation of celebrities. They take the cult of awe and worship to new heights of banality. Or, rather, they simply highlight the cult of worship of fame which exists throughout the media. *Hello!* magazine simply reveals what every other part of the global media does anyway. The tabloids slavishly dog and sensationalize the lives of the famous, and TV and radio too thrive on notions of 'fame' and 'celebrity'.

A new magazine, *Atlanta,* was launched in December, 1995. It was not intended to be a 'woman's magazine' in the *Cosmo* vein, with tips on how to pleasure your man in bed, but a mix of 'serious' issues, 'bold reporting on sex, politics and culture' according to founding editor Nikkie du Preez. *Atlanta* aimed to use the 'worthier elements of *Marie Claire* with 'the style of *Vanity Fair*'. Advance orders for *Atlanta* were 50,000 – small compared to the readerships of *Marie Claire* and *Cosmopolitan* (455,109 and 456,131 respectively, at the time). The staff of five plus the editor were aiming for 100,000. What was unusual about *Atlanta* was that all the profits went to war victims, via the publisher and charity the Atlanta Trust,[11]

Looks (circ. 231,000) is another 'young' 'women's magazine' (aimed at 15-22 year old women [B. Turner, ib, 261]), which focuses almost entirely on fashion and health and hair and how people 'look'. Like the other glossy monthlies, *Looks* trades entirely on the notion of 'looking good', of improving oneself in the realm of fashion-conscious imagery. Other magazines, like *Looks*, base their editorial content almost completely on the importance of looks: *Hair* (bi-monthly, circ. 168,000), *Hair Flair,* and *Slimming. Slimming* (circ. 250,000) is just as insidious as *Hair, The*

---

11 Meg Carter: "Shelf Life", *The Independent*, 12 December 1995, 17

Clothes Show, Looks and *Vogue,* and all 'women's magazines' in its assumptions about the way people look. The very title of the magazine, *Slimming*, like *Weight Watcher's Magazine*, emphasizes the patriarchal nature of the magazine: *Slimming* suggests not the importance of diet and health, but slimming. In other words, losing weight to please one's readings of culture's/ society's notions of the 'slim' person. Much of the 'women's magazine' market concerns 'looking good', which often means conforming to a stereotype of 'beauty' and body shape/ size.

Like *Smash Hits* (which sells close to 400,000 a fortnight), *Just Seventeen* is one of the biggest selling of the mid-teenage market (circ. 244,000; 12-18 year olds [B. Turner, ib, 258]), and concentrates on fashion, image, pop and TV and movie stars, and BOYS, BOYS, BOYS. The heterosexist dominance of boys, boys, boys also features prominently in *Jackie* (circ. 80,000), plus school, friends, fashion, and other aspects of 'growing up'. *Catch* is a teenage magazine that aims to 'go beyond the beauty and personality profile pages' of other teenage magazines (B. Turner, ib., 229) but does not appear much different. Other magazines of this teen type include *Blue Jeans* and *Patches* (from D.C. Thomson).

Just Seventeen and *Mizz* were aimed at 17-18 year olds, women who had grown out of photo love and teeny bopper magazines and who, in the cynical words of marketing controller Stephen Parnell, were 'not ready for home-making, divorce and Greenham Common' (B. Braithwaite, 77). This 'in-betweener' market, between teenage and the so-called 'freedom years' and 'young motherhood', is a lucrative market, as *Mizz, Just Seventeen, Smash Hits* and others have found.

Youth and teenage magazines of the 1970s included *Look Now, Oh Boy!, Honey, 19, Mates, Pink, Mirabelle, My Guy, Hi!, OK* and *Fab 208.* In the history of the various mergers of magazines, *Fab Hits* was launched as *Fab* (1964), and incorporated *Boyfriend* (1966), *Intro* (1976), *Trend* (1976), *Petticoat* (1975), *Hi!* (1976), *OK* (1977) and was merged into *Oh Boy!* in 1980, and then into *My Guy. Woman & Home* absorbed *Good Life* (1980), *My Home & Family* (1971), *Everywoman* (1967), *Modern Woman* and *Modern Home* (1951). *19* incorporated *Honey* (1986), *Vanity Fair* (1972) and *Woman & Beauty* (1963).

Cosmopolitan also has affinities with the magazines aimed at young mothers and parents, such as *Mother and Baby* (circ. 109,061), *Maternity and Mothercraft* (130,000) and *Parents* (circ. 70,000). These are (relatively new) magazines that discuss birth and parenthood from a consumerist point of view, where commodities are very prominent. The sort of content in *Love Story* (circ. 40,000), *Loving* (circ. 22,000), *True Story, True Romances, Woman's Story* and *Loving* (circ. 45,000), which feature 'romantic fiction', appears in *Cosmo*, usually towards the back, in the 'short fiction' slot. Three titles, however – *True Romances, Love Story* and *True Story* have been withdrawn, after their 'combined monthly circulation fell below 50,000'.[12] In magazines such as *Just Seventeen* (as well as 'older' 'women's magazines', such as *Best* and *Woman's Own*), the hegemony of meta-narratives of romance have been replaced by 'blip publishing', the snippets of info about pop stars, celebs, soaps *et al.* Readers now desire sex, celebrity and crime, it's claimed, so titles such as *Chat, Celebrity* and *True Crime* are booming.

House & Garden (circ. 144,000), *Homes and Gardens* (circ. 206, 000), *House Beautiful* (circ. 271,319), *The World of Interiors* (circ. 73,210), *Home and Country, Garden News* (circ. 114,564), *Country Living* (circ. 175,000) and *Practical Gardening* (107,730) also feed into 'women's magazines' territory. All 'women's magazines' feature items on the house, whether a country cottage, or a town house with mock Victorian four poster beds and window boxes. The lovely lovely photographs of luxurious interiors in the above mentioned magazines are found in all 'women's magazines'. The consumerism of all 'women's magazines', of all magazines, is nowhere more apparent than in these detailed, brightly-lit, high-colour stills of beautiful homes. It's the gleaming, neat and so-smug face of Western capitalism.

The biggest sellers in the magazine market are often those based around the home/ garden/ family/ and 'women's' market, such as *Good House-keeping* (circ. 381,450), a magazine of recipes, health, style and interior

---

12 Jon Ronson: "All Passion Spent", *The Independent*, 27 September 1994, 24

design, *Woman's Realm* (circ. 483,000), *Prima* (circ. 738,871), *The People's Friend* (circ. 566,000), which describes itself as 'a good read for all the family' (B. Turner, 273), *Me* (circ. 600,000), *Take a Break* (circ. 1.3 million) which appears on supermarket check-out racks, alongside *TV Times* and *Woman, Woman's Own* (circ. 931,295), *Weekly News* (circ. 487,606), *Woman's Weekly* (circ. 905,095), *More* (circ. 262,000), *My Weekly* (696,279), *Best* (circ. 660,000), *Bella* (circ. 1.3 million), and *Family Circle* (circ. 406,190).

Woman's Realm, relaunched in 1982, took on the concept of 'blip publishing' in 1987 (short, colourful items for quick, easy reading). The target audience was, editor Judith Hall admitted, the 'Oxo mum', the housewife who 'wanted good value for money' (B. Braithwaite, 72). *Family Circle* is one of the more 'traditional' of 'women's magazines', while *Essentials* (circ. 519,000) is a *Woman*-style populist magazine (recipes, fashion, soap and TV stars, personal stories), that also includes a 'free' knitting/ sewing pattern each month, so that customers buy the magazine 'for the pattern'. The British Broadcasting Corporation entered the women's consumer magazine market with *BBC Good Food* (491,178) and *The Clothes Show Magazine. Annabel*, though the title might suggest another teenage magazine such as *Jackie*, is 'currently aimed at women aged 35 and over' (B. Turner, ib, 219), that is, the *Family Circle/ Woman's Realm* market.

More recent ABC (Audit Bureau Circulation) figures, for 2009: *More* 190,000, *Grazia* 228,000, *Yours* 301,000, *Heat* 445,000, *Closer* 530,000, *Top Sante* 85,000, *Mother and Baby* 60,000, *FHM* 235,000, *GQ* 179,000, and *Zoo* 111,000.

Other 'women's magazines' of the 1960s to the present day include: *Kin, Glamour, Going Shopping, Good Life, Child's Play, Embroidery, Diana, Country Homes & Interiors, Harpers Bazaar, Heartbeat, Home Chat, Hers, Here's Health, Ideal Home, Flair, Home & Freezer Digest, Home Companion, Home and Family, Getting Married, Green Cuisine, Hair & Good Looks Book, Hair Care, Freezer Family, Girl About Town, Girl Monthly, Fashion, Oh Boy!, Fashion Folio, Fashioncraft, Fashion and*

*Craft, Everywoman, Extra-Special, Fab Hits, Love Affair, Fiz, Food
Magazine, Celebrity, Caroline, Health & Fitness, Slimmer, Blue Jeans,
Candida, True Love, Brides & Setting Up Home, Beauty & Skincare,
Baby Magazine, Boyfriend, Beauty & Hair, Lady Gossip, Looking Good,
Living, Lipstick, Loving Weekly, Machine Knitting News, Photo Secret
Love, Petticoat, Pins and Needles, Home Improvements Guides, Image,
Home Notes, Keep Fit Magazine, Romeo, Patches, Knit & Stitch, In Store,
Parents, Roxy, Mates, Marty, Marilyn, Mirabelle, Store, Intro, Inhabit, M
& S Magazine, Parent Care, Office Secretary, Nursery World, Nova,
Modern Woman, Valentine, Vogue Patterns, Trend, True, True Monthly,
True Romances, Traditional Kitchens Magazine, Womancraft with
Sewing and Knitting, Woman Bride and Home, What Diet & Lifestyle, W,
Woman's Mirror, Woman's Day, Woman and Home, Woman's
Illustrated, Woman's Story, Woman's Way, Women's Review, World of
Knitting, Young Mother, Your Baby, Working Woman, Woman's Friend,
Romance, Successful Slimming, Style Magazine, Tomorrow, Riva,
Queen, The Townswoman, Traditional Homes* and *Your Hair.*

Good Housekeeping encourages us to 'BE YOURSELF' on the cover of its
April, 1994 issue. *Good Housekeeping* is a magazine, male anti-feminists
would say, for the housewife as mousewife. Not much feminism in *Good
Housekeeping*; instead, good housekeepers. Its material centres around the
home, a cosy notion of what homelife is all about. Features include money
at home (how to make it), adultery, divorce without tears ('is it really
possible?'), and life in a commune (showing the alternative to the
'traditional' kind of homelife). The genres of articles in *Good Housekeeping* are the staple ones of 'women's magazines': health, travel, gardens,
fashion and beauty, fiction and celebrities. *Good Housekeeping*, at first
glance, is simply a glossy version of the women's weeklies. In magazines
such as *Good Housekeeping* and *Woman's Own*, women are called
'housewives' without any irony or self-consciousness. For instance, in an
article on smacking children, the general public is interviewed: we read a
few lines of text from people giving their views on hitting kids: we hear
from 'Joanna Attewell, 27, housewife', 'Nigel Lewsey, 31, engineer',

'COSMO WOMAN'

'Jeanette Morillon, 34, housewife'.[13]

In *Woman's Journal* there is an article on the 1980s 'New Man' (that is, the 'feminine' man who does housework, looks after the kids, is sympathetic, etc). The piece has a quiz: 'how much of a woman is your man?' is the leading question. The other questions are the usual trite, bland questions of 'women's (and all) magazines':

does he worry about his appearance?... is he in touch with his emotions?... does he try too hard to please?

These are the questions which the writer thinks are qualities 'feminine' men have.[14] The questions circulate around stereotypical views of women, of women's view of women, of men's view of women.

Premiere, Empire, Sight and Sound, and *Film Monthly,*[15] the film review magazines, like most pop magazines, aim much of their material at a masculinist audience. Or, if they don't intentionally target a masculinist audience, their magazines are mainly masculinist in content and meaning. Nearly all 'film buffs', whether on telly in bland review shows such as *Film* (BBC), *The Little Picture Show, Cinema, Cinema, Cinema* or *Hollywood Report,* on children's TV, or on discussions on radio arts programmes, are male, or masculinist in bias. 'Women's magazines', of all kinds, thrive on the entertainment industry, from TV soap stars to movie and pop stars. As most 'women's magazines' use the 'personality profile' approach, in the form of interviews or pieces on Hollywood gossip (who's directing whom in what), film criticism in 'women's magazines' is based entirely on personalities. The more 'sophisticated' film criticism in *Screen* or *Sight and Sound* becomes in 'women's magazines' a series of stills from the film and movie stars interviews. The 'serious'/ scholarly approach of the film journals becomes the bland exaltation of stars and personalities in general

13 Angela Goodwin: "Smacking: You the parents have your say", *Woman's Own*, 6 January 1992, 26-27
14 Lynn Pierce: "How Much of a Woman is Your Man?", *Woman's Journal*, March 1994, 40-41
15 ABC figures for 2009: *Empire* 194,000, *Total Film* 85,000, and *Sight & Sound* 19,700.

interest and 'women's magazines'.

Sky is a 'style' magazine that appears to straddle the border between 'women's magazines', style magazines and the music press. Like *The Face*, *GQ* and *Arena*, *Sky* incorporates elements of fashion, sport, media, music, Hollywood, as well as pop music. A look at *Sky*'s cover reveals the following cover-lines:

OBSCENELY HIGHLY-PAID FOOTBALLERS
SUMMER'S HOT STONED LOVE MOVIE *DAZED AND CONFUSED*
MISSION IMPOSSIBLE: ROAD-TESTING LUDICROUS SEX TIPS
HOW TO BE A GUN NUTTER
(*Sky*, September, 1994)

Sky's cover shows 'supermodel' Claudia Schiffer topless, on a beach, wet in the surf, kneeling, clutching her boobs, just about covering her nipples. It's one of the classic poses of softcore pornography and pin-up photography. Increasingly throughout the 1980s and 1990s the style and fashion magazines looked like print versions of youth TV shows, mixing fashion and celebrity interviews with sensational topics such as guns, video violence, sex, rape, etc.

The weekly pop 'newspapers', *New Musical Express* (circ. 115,000 in 1994, 41,000 in 2009) and *Melody Maker* (71,900 in 1994, now defunct), assume a largely masculinist audience. The presentation and prose of the weekly pop papers, like most pop radio, including BBC Radio 1, Kiss FM, Atlantic 252, Laser 558, Radio Luxembourg, etc, produces masculinist/ patriarchal views and attitudes. Though women may buy the pop newspapers and magazines (*Vox, Select, Mojo, Q*),[16] the masculinist dimension is always uppermost. Though women may be part of the audience of the pop magazines, pop remains very much a masculinist media. The pop magazines that stress fandom and adulation (*Smash Hits, Just Seventeen*) are firmly associated with 'teeny boppers', i.e., the young women that scream at Radio 1 roadshows, at the Beatles at airports, at Bay

---

16 2009 ABC figures for the music press: *Q* 100,000, *Mojo* 97,000 and 70,000 for *Classic Rock*.

City Rollers concerts, etc.

There has, since the 1980s, been a rise in the number of 'men's magazines' that are not the usual 'men's' magazines', i.e., pornography. Though these 'new' 'men's magazines' include porn, they are based on the 'style' magazines of the early 1980s: *The Face, i-D* and *Blitz*. The trend, of *The Face, Blitz, i-D* and *Elle*, the 'style' magazines, has been towards a postmodernist emphasis on surface, where the world is flattened out, and trivia and profundity, surface and depth, are placed on the same plane. The design of the 'style-ographers' (as Neville Brody and his fellow designers were called)[17] rules supreme. The 'new' 'men's magazines' – *GQ, Arena, Esquire* – are, like all magazines, firmly based in consumerism and the advertizing network of chat show interviews. The usual products are puffed up: books, movies, CDs, buildings, concerts. Interviews, as always, are structured around forthcoming films or TV shows. The notions of masculinity produced by the 'new' 'men's magazines' turns out to be extremely narrow, boiling down to the categories of Sunday newspapers: fashion, cars, lifestyle, health, entertainment, etc. How boring the press is, the media is. It squeezes articles into genres and categories. So much is decided by these genres. If you've got something that'll fit in with this month's splash on ritual child abuse, great. If not, forget it.

The fashion spreads and ads in magazines such as *i-D, Elle, Arena, GQ* and *The Face* feature pouting, self-conscious people, self-consciously scruffy, scuzzy, dirty, snarling, disaffected. These people are shown hanging around street corners, or in dingy bars, eyes downcast, in surly, post-teenage moody angst. In the style press, such as in *i-D*, sex is used to sell products in the usual way, but often with added political, ideological, self-conscious and stylish elements. In the ad for Diesel jeans, a large black-and-white picture of a man holding a gun at the viewer is put behind a colour shot of a young model wearing cut-off jeans, complete with emphasized cleavage. Two aspects of sexuality and culture are juxtaposed here: male violence, embodied forcefully in the gun, and vulnerable femininity, in the woman staring at the viewer with her lipsticked pout and prominent breasts. The copy for this ad is a short paragraph in the style

17 "The Stylographers", Radio 4 documentary, 29 Sept 1988

familiar from magazines such as *The Face, i-D, Arena, GQ* and *Blitz*:

> MODERN CHILDREN need to solve their *OWN* problems: teaching kids
> to KILL helps them deal *directly* with reality – but they learn SO much
> quicker when you give them a guiding hand! Make them proud and
> confident![18]

While magazines such as *Cosmopolitan* and *Just Seventeen* sell in
(relatively) large numbers, it is worth keeping in mind that many other
magazines of a quite different content also sell hundreds of thousands of
copies each week and month: *Farmers Weekly* (circ. 265,000), *Farming
News* (circ. 102,000), *Practical Photography* (110,040), *Autocar & Motor*
(circ. 96,500), *Computer Weekly* (112, 000), *Angling Times* (126,155),
Shooting and Conservation (110,000), *The Sporting Life* (circ. 95,181),
Motor Cycle News (circ. 139,385), *Moneywise* (circ. 96,000), *Camping
and Caravanning* (96, 528), *Business Life* (circ. 110,000), and
pornography, such as *Club International* (180,000), *Penthouse* (circ.
100,000), and *Mayfair* (331,760). The 'church' or 'Christian' magazines
also sell very well, in the hundreds of thousands: *The Sign* and *The
Universe.*

If these figures are accurate, someone somewhere is making a lot of
money from magazines.

'Women's magazines' cluster around certain aspects of lifestyle or
fashion. There are the foodie mags (*Taste, Cooks Weekly, A la Carte*),
brides to be (*Wedding & Home, Brides & Setting Up Home*), young
mothers (*Mother & Baby, Parents, Practical Parenting, Mother*), the
home (*Ideal Home, Homes & Gardens, Good Housekeeping, House &
Garden*), fashion and style (*Vogue, Elle*), slimming and health (*Slimming,
Weight Watchers, Zest*), hair (*Hair Care, Hair, Hair Flair*) and so on.
Each aspect of that nebulous concept termed 'woman' has its own group of
magazines. The market for magazines aimed at men's interests, hobbies and
pleasures is much greater than in the realm of 'women's magazines'. There
are magazines about the masculine pursuits of keeping pigeons, fishing,
kart racing, off-road driving, classic car building, yachting, windsurfing,

---

18 *i-D*, no. 114, March 1993, 72-73

mountain climbing, chess, cricket, football, etc.

A useful way of comparing the 'women's magazines' studied here is to look at the median age of the female readership. *Cosmo*'s readership is 27.3 years old on average: *Just Seventeen* is 17.5 (readers start at 13 and hang on until age 18 and over, says David Hepworth, editorial director of EMAP Metro), *Jackie* is 19.9, *Over 21* is 22.8, *Elle* is 24.1, *Company* is 24.4, *Options* is 29.3, *Vogue* is 32.1, *Woman* is 37.3, *She* is 37.5, *Woman's Own* is 37.8, *Family Circle* is 39.1, *Woman's Journal* is 44.8 and *The People's Friend* is 58.6 (B. Braithwaite, 96).

Who is the reader of 'women's magazines'? The editor of *Prima* (Sue James) said the *Prima* reader was practical, married, with a family, with interests such as cooking, knitting, homecraft and fashion. *Woman and Home*'s readership, according to its editor, wants innovative ideas for cooking, stylish ideas for home decoration and good fiction. Jill Churchill, editor of *Family Circle*, says the reader is lonely: the magazine has to be peopled with friendly faces, so it acts as a companion to the lonely reader. Readers were particularly hungry for features related to children. *Woman's Weekly*'s editor Judith Hall also perceives her magazine as a friend: *Woman's Weekly* is 'friendly and unashamedly homely'. Finally, *Cosmopolitan*'s editor of the 1980s (Linda Kelsey) said that the '*Cosmo* girl' has evolved into a 'highly sophisticated young woman': she owns an apartment, has a career, is more affluent, and is or wants to be in a relationship (B. Braithwaite, 141-6).

The sameness of many magazines, women's or otherwise, is not explained by the fact that many personnel have worked on each other's magazines, that editors go to the same lunches and press parties, that they use the same writers. It is more to do with the audience, which is hungry for more... of the same. Every day three million or so readers in the U.K. buy *The Sun* newspaper: it has pretty much the same sort of content day in day out, yet every day three million or so people buy it. Similarly with 'women's magazines': the content may not vary much, but it seems to satisfy some hunger in the audience. Hunger for what? Information, gossip, identification, entertainment, news, etc. Reassurance? Friendship?

Magazines are a panoply of contrasts. In *Elle* we flip from a double page ad for Calvin Klein's perfume *Eternity*, which shows a young white middle-class woman joyfully embracing her five year-old daughter on a windswept beach, to, on the next page, a 'serious' article, "Why women don't initiate sex".[19] This article quotes 'real' people, in the usual manner: short pieces of data with no surnames:

> If the two of you argue [says Mary Ellen], a man will always try and make up by initiating sex, which annoys women. If he's got the energy to have sex, why doesn't he have the energy to try and solve the problem? (ib., 17)

Next page, a double page ad for Nike showing in soft focus six nude women, one with a baby – images of archetypal 'female beauty'. Next page, a feature, full of colour pictures of 'aggressive' young women, i.e., fashion models, who are the 'new nasty girls'.[20] The pictures show women in 'masculine' poses, representations of 'assertive' women, the sort of images where women are labelled 'dykes' or lesbians.

Fashion magazines are cyclical: the same articles are regurgitated 20 million different ways. Thus, in September, 1993's *Elle*, there is a piece on the colour black,[21] the colour fashion designers the world over love. How many articles have we seen on black, or on the 'little black dress'? This article on black allows all those old transparencies or JPEG files to be pulled out of the draw marked 'FOR FUTURE REFERENCE'. We see shots of (yawn) Sean Connery as James Bond (black suit), Audrey Hepburn, Michelle Pffeifer as Cat Woman from the 'black' *Batman* movies, and pop bands such as The Cure and Siouxsie and the Banshees (black 'Goth' fashion), the Velvet Underground (black leather jackets) and Gary Numan. This is one of the most obvious forms of repetition which keeps the media alive. Black, mini skirts, long hair, bad skin, animal welfare, Christmas

---

19 Dylan Jones: "Why women don't initiate sex", *Elle*, September 1993, 17
20 Sarah Broene: "The rise of the nasty girls", *Elle*, September 1993, 20-22
21 Kathy Philips: "Black", *Elle*, September 1993, 63-66

dinner, these things return *ad nauseam*. Humans certainly *love* repetition. They would die without it.

Elle, seemingly so stylish, offers the same product as the more 'downmarket' weekly magazines, only 'better' crafted. For instance, *Elle* has articles on mother-daughter relationships, on health and beauty, on food and interiors, just the same as *Woman's Own* or *Bella*. The fashion magazines appear to be more 'stylish' simply because of their 'superior' or 'trendier' graphics. The concept of 'womanhood'/ 'femininity' in the 'high class' fashion magazines – *Vogue, Tatler, Marie Claire, Elle, Harpers & Queen* – is basically the same as that in the more staid, domestic 'women's magazines'. It is the same stereotypes that are (re)presented: images of women as vixens, or whores, or viragoes, as good or bad mothers, as trendy or dowdy people, as socialites or stay-at-homes.

Elle's August, 1994 issue has a cover which contains the usual mix of stereotypical 'womanhood' or 'femininity':

SEX AND STRESS – THE NEW BED PARTNERS
THE MEN WHO UNDERSTAND WOMEN
THE BEST BEAUTY KITS
WHY SEX AND GLAMOUR ARE BACK

This last menu taster, 'WHY SEX AND GLAMOUR ARE BACK' is typical of the cyclical nature of all 'women's magazines', of all magazines. The idea that sexuality and glamour 'are back' is a form of lie, for they have never been 'away', and especially not for a style magazine. After all, every issue of *Elle, Cosmopolitan, Marie Claire* and *all* other 'women's magazines' are founded on the institutionalizations of sexuality and glamour.

In February, 1994's *Marie Claire* there are features on 'blind dates', where two 'real life' people meet for the first time, and talk about their meetings. It is a superficial feature, where the people involved discuss the looks, appearance, tastes and hates of their blind date. 'He had nice hair' or 'the film he liked was important' are typical comments.[22] Glenda Bailey was

---

22 Deborah Holder: "The Date: How It Went: Review: Man of the Month", *Marie Claire*, February 1994, 50

the outspoken, interferring, Northern British editor of *Marie Claire*, who helped launch the British edition of the French magazine in 1988. Glenda Bailey cleverly encouraged a forceful mix of 'briskly treated sex, third world horror stories, and lavish fashion and beauty', which helped the readership to rise.[23] The combination of supposedly 'hard-hitting' journalistic reportage and high fashion chic began to take the fire away from other high fashion magazines such as *Vogue, Elle* and *Cosmopolitan* (seen as *Marie Claire*'s main competitors), so that, by the mid-1990s, *Marie Claire* was the biggest selling high fashion 'women's magazine', with a circulation of more than 450,000.

Marie Claire did not do anything that had not already been done in 'women's magazine' publishing. There had been stories of bizarre sexual practices for ages, and 'serious' reporting from around the world. The 'serious' journalistic features were problematic for advertizers, who did not always like having their ads appearing beside such downbeat editorial material. The 'serious' reportage gave *Marie Claire* an apparent edge over other magazines, for it showed that the magazine was not simply devoted to 'trivial' things, such as beauty or shopping. The reportage flattered the audience into thinking they were consuming something 'substantial' and 'worthy'. *Marie Claire* could not be dismissed as a trashy, fluffy, lightweight read, because it tackled 'serious' issues.

Looks (April, 1994) tells us that 'it's raining men', a startling idea which comes from a feature on 'sixteen of the horniest new male models'.[24] In this feature, colour and black-and-white photographs are set beside mini-biographies, where the male models are described in terms of age, height, eyes, place of birth, star sign, their 'fave model', their 'big dream', their 'passions' and their 'bad habits'. Here it is assumed that the male models' 'fave model' will be female: i.e., Cindy Crawford, Yasmin Le Bon, Christy Turlington, Claudia Schiffer, etc.

Many (most) 'women's magazines' investigate men in their features. What are men like, what (and how) do they think, what they wear, what they desire. For 'women's magazines', men are the main target in the single

23 Suzi Feay: "What she wants", *The Independent on Sunday*, 21 January 1995
24 Scarlett Brady: "It's raining men", *Looks* April 1994, 22-24

heterosexual woman's search for happiness (embodied in a heterosexual relationship). So 'women's magazines' are full of articles by men about men, and by women about men, made for an audience of mainly women who are thought to be interested in men. Old stereotypes are trotted out (that 'older men' are handsome, for instance). Articles on 'old' men include pictures of Sean Connery, Mick Jagger, Clint Eastwood, and so on.[25] 'Women's magazines' worry over issues such as men and adultery: why do they do it? Or men and money: why don't they let you spend it? Or men and impotence: why they won't admit to it.[26] One of the most enduring topics concerning men discussed in 'women's magazines' is: why do men bottle up their feelings? Why can't they be like women, highly emotional and expressive? Why, 'women's magazines' persist, do men talk passionately about football and cars but not about love and emotions? In an article entitled "Why do men have mates not friends?" the author muses:

They'll talk politics and porn...but they won't use the F word. Feelings, that is. [27]

In *Clothes Show* (November, 1992), the rigours of heterosexuality and stereotyping is at its strongest. The article "Men: What they think of what you wear" has a group of men (five white, one black) who 'judge' what one model wears. She wears five different outfits, each one under a heading: there is 'College Girl', with flat shoes, suede trousers and a white skirt. 'She's a little bit preppy [the copy describes her], a little bit sporty, wholesome in a fresh faced sort of way'. Next to 'College Girl' is 'Frankly Feminine' woman, and we are told that 'Julia Roberts is her idol. She's feminine but no sissy – look how far she's unbuttoned her dress!' 'Frankly Feminine' woman is wearing a printed cotton dress. 'Class Act' woman is 'a vamp': '[s]he's one classy act and knows it. You can look but don't touch unless invited to.' She is wearing a black sidesplit full-length dress, and a red jacket, with big Hollywood hair: 'dressed to kill' is the telling common

25 Jo Foley: "Mature Attraction", *Chic*, March/ April 1994, 48-51
26 "A woman's guide to Impotence", *Cosmopolitan*, July 1994
27 Jon Courtenay: "Why do men have mates not friends?", *New Woman*, June 1994, 186

phrase. 'Working Girl' is, the copy runs, 'heading for the top but she likes to work and play.' She is wearing a light cream trouser suit, her hair is pulled back, with a patterned scarf. 'Fashion Victim' woman is a '[d]ancing Queen. She's fashion mad and ready to party.'

The men in the ruthlessly stereotypical and reductive *Clothes Show* article are described as 'The Boxer', 'The Pop Star', 'The Actor', 'The Soul Star', 'The Photographer' and 'The Model'. They describe 'Frankly Feminine' woman as 'very attractive...a wolf in sheep's clothing...quite sexy'. The 'vamp' ('Class Act'), the most obviously 'sexy' (i.e., whorish looking), is described as 'definitely my favourite' by 'The Boxer'. 'This woman's dressed to kill' gushes 'The Pop Star', while 'The Photographer' makes the obvious statement about rape: '[t]his is the 'I'm begging for it' look'. 'The Actor', meanwhile, admits the 'vamp' is '[a] definite winner', and 'The Soul Star' says '[d]efinitely very sexy'. 'The Model' states '[s]he's sexy and she knows it.'[28] What this photo feature bluntly reveals are the usual social stereotypes of women, where women who dress as a 'vamp' are 'begging for it', 'it' being of course a fuck. Unsurprisingly, all the men looking at the 'vamp', 'Class Act', remark on her sexiness, and stress her sexual availability.

Cosmopolitan is (relatively) unusual in that women occupy many of the top jobs on the magazine. Generally, women inhabit a small proportion of the higher echelons of broadcasting and media management. At magazines such as *Just Seventeen* and *Smash Hits,* the EMAP Metro stars, there are many producers vieing for power: journalists, photographers, advertizers, the music industry: the relationships between these groups of people are played out across the pages of the magazines.[29] Though the staff on some 'women's magazines' are not mainly male, the strategies and ideologies are usually masculinist. In the A & R departments of record companies, most A & R people are male, while the secretaries and personal assistants, the ones who do much of the drudgery (making tea, filing, typing, phoning) are

28 Saska Graville: "Men: What they think of what you wear!", *Clothes Show* magazine, November 1992, 12-18
29 Helen Pleasance: "Open or Closed: popular magazines and dominant culture", in Franklin, 1992, 79-80

female (K. Negus, 58). There is, for instance, a 'BBC person', a 'BBC sort of person', someone who will 'fit in' with the structure of the British Broadcasting Corportation. The ideal BBC person is, of course, male.[30] In Britain's independent television sector, 12 out of 306 camera operators were women (in 1986), and there were 19 women out of 1,395 engineers.[31] In the BBC in 1985 at the top grade of personnel there were 6 women and 159 men.[32] Among BBC governors, over ten years 'only 7 out of 34' have been women.[33] These are not as enlightened times as we would like to think: women can't be taken seriously if they're beautiful.[34]

According to magazines such as *Woman's Realm, Woman's Weekly, Family Circle, Essentials, Me, Bella* and *Prima*, what women want to read about is recipes, cookery, health, beauty, fashion, personal profiles of soap and movie stars, and gardening. Few things are as offensive as the assumptions about their audiences made by the editors and writers of these more 'traditional' and 'cosy' 'women's magazines'. Do the people who buy 'women's magazines' such as *Woman's Journal, Take a Break, Country Living, Prima* and *Best really* want to read about these topics? Editors and publishers in the U.K. (H. Bauer Publishing, G & J (UK), National Magazine Company, IPC Magazines Ltd, Condé Nast Publications, EMAP, Hearst Group) might laugh all the way to the bank, and reply, of course they do. For the cosy, 'traditional', populist 'women's magazines' sell by the hundreds of thousands each week.

For critics (usually male), the banality of the content of 'women's magazines', the recipes, beauty, fashion, etc, affirms their view of the insipidity of 'women's culture' in general, and perhaps even of women. While men read about big, aggressive topics, such as global politics, or militia, or guns, or cars, women read about adultery, cookery, and beauty tips. 'Women's culture', as expressed in 'women's magazines', is distinctly

---

30 S. Hood. *On Television*, Pluto Press, London, 1980, 28-29.
31 Anne Rose Muir: "The Status of Women Working in Film and Television", in L. Gamman, 144; Sarah Benton: "Patterns of Discrimination Against Women in the Film and Television Industries", *Film and Television Technician*, March 1975
32 Monica Smith, *Women in BBC Management*, BBC, 1985
33 Nigel Willmot, "Who's Running Broadcasting?", *Broadcast*, 13 February 1987, 22-23
34 Margaret Marshment: "Substantial Women", in L. Gamman, 37

in 'second place', when compared by some critics with 'men's culture'. It's the same with local and daytime radio shows, which copy the format of 'women's magazines' with their gardening, recipe, keep-fit, legal and celebrity slots. Radio, however, is 'overwhelmingly a male domain' (S. Barnard, 1989, 143), with men in most of the key managerial positions. That has changed a little more recently.

The 'women's magazines' that think of themselves as more 'cutting edge' and 'serious' (*Marie Claire, Cosmopolitan, Elle*) than the cosy health-and-recipe magazines (*Best, Prima, Woman's Realm*) publish stories of 'bizarre' or 'unusual' sex acts and views. In this respect, they are no different from the British newspaper tabloids (*The Sun, Daily Star, News of the World, Sunday People, Daily Mail, Daily Express, Daily Mirror*), which often feature stories such as:

COCAINE MADE ME SEX-MAD LESBIAN

Page three favourite Kirsten Imria has revealed how a secret craving for cocaine turned her into a sex-crazed lesbian.

(*News of the World*, 16 October, 1994)

However, most of the populist, moral majority 'housewife' magazines (*Prima, Woman's Own, Bella*, etc) also run features on 'weird' sex, running from the ubiquitous 'my son told me he was homosexual' to sex changes and genital grafts. It's no good saying that these populist products ('women's magazines', soap operas, tabloid newspapers) pander to the 'lowest common denominator', or that they churn out near-garbage, because, the editors and publishers will say, people buy 'em in droves. When critics complain that sensationalizing tabloids sell too many copies for society's good, publishers and newspaper owners reply, smugly, *well, why don't they stop buying them, then?*

Cosmopolitan and other magazines (such as *Options*) do have their sections for men: *Cosmo Man* and *OM*. However, these magazines 'borrow as much from *Playboy* and *Gentleman's Quarterly*, with their emphasis on power, money, business, sporting and sexual success for white, middle-class men, as they do on any New Man ideology' (J. Winship, 1987, 153). Similarly, by the mid-1990s, magazines for men sported more soft porn features than any to do with 'sensitive' men. Not 'New Men' magazines, they were 'New Lads', a.k.a. 'lad mags' (*Loaded, Sky, GQ, Arena, Esquire*).

Men don't have anything remotely similar to 'women's magazines', to *Woman's Realm, Cosmopolitan, She, Family Circle* or *Harpers & Queen*. Only in the 1980s were there 'men's magazines' that aimed to discuss emotional or 'life' problems. In pornography, for example problems are not welcomed, for porn is fantasy, and must be blameless, valueless, guiltless, 'free'. Only rarely do 'serious' reader's problems get an airing in pornography. Other than that, there is no equivalent for men of the agony column. Magazines aimed at men have always centred around genres, and the problems addressed have always been projected outwards, i.e., to do with cameras or cars, fishing tackle or football.

Only in the 1980s did 'men's magazines' appear that were based on more general interest magazines, although *Arena, GQ, Esquire*, etc, were very much fashion and style products. Men, or rather, usually boys, do write to agony columns occasionally, voicing their 'relationship' problems, but they are definitely in a tiny minority. It is women, not men, who have created a magazine culture of emotional/ psychological responses, in the agony column. Or rather, it is 'women's culture' hollowed out from within masculinist/ patriarchal culture that has addressed directly emotional problems. '

Women's magazines' create a world of companionship, solidarity, advice and information quite different from the solidarity and 'brotherhood' in 'men's magazines'. While 'men's magazines' discuss the finer points of radio antennae or the right sort of feed for racing pigeons, 'women's magazines' have created a network of problem-solving that looks at emotional, financial, psychological, social, marital and political issues. While 'women's magazines', it's true, hardly ever stray near the crucial issue of race, and often give idiotically simplistic answers to complex issues, they do nevertheless provide a platform where issues can be raised. Here, though they are carefully edited and selected before being published, the reader's views can be expressed. As with all magazines and newspapers, the reader's letters page and the agony column are vital. Here we discover some of the reader's criticisms and joys in the consumption of the media.

2

THE 'COSMO WOMAN'

COVERS AND HEADLINES

LET'S start with the typical front page of *Cosmopolitan*. As with most other 'women's magazines', *Cosmopolitan* features a woman, a model, smiling. It's not a movie star, or someone with a name (the model, we see inside, is called 'Rohini'. Models/ supermodels are known by their first names: Naomi, Claudia, Kate). The imagery of the woman is 'positive', 'exuberant', 'young', 'tanned', 'smart', 'in control', 'self-confident'. The photographs on the covers of 'women's magazines' speak of healthy living, clean-washed clothes, where white is truly sparkling white. Teeth are perfect. There are no wrinkles or unsightly flabby bits of skin. The models' skin is blemishless. Jewellry is perfect and there are no 'bad hair' days for cover stars. This woman is nameless but she is also '*Cosmo* woman', centrepiece of the image selected to sell this month's issue of the magazine. The model is chosen to portray the mood and aims of the magazine, and to leap out of the other magazines on the racks. She is, of course, also the mirror of the audience, but a stylized, idealized mirror. The cover of *Cosmo* shows the would-be buyer and audience what they *could* be like.

It is a piece of advertizing, the magazine cover. It invites the browser into the world of the magazine. It has to make a direct and instantaneous appeal to the potential buyer. Booksellers know that the most important aspect of a book's sales potential is its cover. Magazines have developed cover design to a refined artform, and each magazine has its house style, its code of subtle laws that consumers interpret in a very sophisticated manner. There may not be much to read on the cover, but it takes a while to really explain and understand the significance of every aspect of a cover. Like a movie poster or a burger bar menu, a magazine cover is a highly stylized product (physical details of the magazine cover include type size, shape and colour; size and texture of paper; the sell-lines; the lay-out; it's also crucial where the magazine is displayed – high or low, or next to particular magazines).

The cover of *Company*'s June, 1983 issue shows a Kate Bush lookalike staring wistfully at the viewer with her head on one side (acres of lipgloss, perfect skin, blusher, big Hollywood hair). The cover-lines are shamelessly positive: 'CHANGE! LEARN TO PLAY THE NEW SHAPE GAME', 'SELF-ESTEEM: A LITTLE MORE WILL TAKE YOU A LONG WAY', and of course the obligatory sex cover line (as usual, first on the left under the title): 'BLISS AND THE SINGLE BED'. The sell-lines of *Options* usually pivot around ways in which home life can be enriched: on *Options*' July, 1983 cover there are sell-lines on 'better fashion', 'better food' and 'better homes'; but the largest sell-line again addresses sex: 'THE NEW JEALOUSY: MUST HE ALWAYS HAVE IT SO GOOD?'

If you, the reader (or 'Derrida' as postmodern comics like to say), wanna look like the cover model of *Cosmopolitan, Company, Marie Claire, Options* and *Best et al,* the information on the contents page of most 'women's magazines' tells you what you'll need to achieve 'the look'. August, 1994 has an astonishing list of items needed for the ultimate makeover into the '*Cosmo* Woman':

Orange swimsuit, Liza Bruce. Yellow towel, Harrods. Recreate this look using Rimmel cosmetics. Complexion: Translucent Moist Make Up in Warm Honey with Pressed Powder in Silky Beige. Cheeks: Sheer Brilliance Cheek & Eye Colour in Fragile Rose. Eyes: Pearly Eyes in Barley Pearls with Eye Liner Pencil in Black Magic, Soft Kohl Pencil in Sable Brown, Active Lash Mascara in Black and Eye Brown Pencil in Black. Lips: Polished Lip Colour in Polished Clear. Nails: French Ivory and Coconut Ice from Rimmel's French Manicure System. (*Cosmopolitan,* August, 1994, 4)

It's a make-up arsenal worthy of a Hollywood blockbuster movie on a day when 2,000 extras are hired.

The *Cosmo* woman has always required a lot of consumer, technological and financial back-up in order to effect the dream make-over from ordinary woman into *Cosmo* 'superwoman'. A competition run early in *Cosmo*'s career (April, 1973), the 'Supergirl contest', emphasized the goal of finding 'the prettiest, best dressed, most *alive* girls around', not a fashion model, but someone with a 'mind'. However, the emphasis was on beauty and looks.

The *Cosmopolitan* cover announces the contents in capitals and lower case coloured type:

LEST WE FORGET Women's greatest power is sexual

'S WONDERFUL, 'S MARVELLOUS
How a man knows he's in love with you

REAR ADMIRABLE Why men are so turned on by women's bottoms

A CONDOM FOR THE HEART The only way to have really safe sex

YOUR MOST PERSONAL SEXUAL EXPERIENCE[35]

Clustered around the main photograph the captions are often two sentences or phrases coupled together: a two-word phrase and another phrase underneath, to explain further, like a headline and a sub-heading. These captions are set in bold type, in different colours: pink, red, yellow, dark blue, light blue, green. These coloured bits of type recall 'youth' magazines, such as the pop magazine *Smash Hits*, or magazines aimed at young women/ girls, *Jackie, Just Seventeen* and *Mizz*. No page of *Cosmo* is dull and grey, It is all zappy stuff, until the 8 or so pages of classified and personal ads at the back of the magazine.

Five of the seven sell-lines on *Cosmo*'s cover are about or related to sex: 'How a man knows he's in love with you', 'Women's greatest power is sexual', 'Gloria Steinem on women's bodies, muscles and men', 'Why men

---

35 *Cosmopolitan*, June 1994; November 1983

are so turned on by women's bottoms' and 'The only way to have really safe sex'. The other two captions on the cover relate to sexual or heterosexual matters: 'WE'RE OUTTA HERE! When he prefers his freedom, his flat, his friends and his football' and 'CRIMES OF VIOLENCE Why they make weak men feel strong'. Here massively complex issues are reduced to their purest media form: the two-second soundbite, the neat, pat phrase.

Here is a selection from some more *Cosmopolitan* front covers:

NOT sleeping with the enemy: how to get the best from a womaniser

LOVE AND SECURITY: When he likes you a little and you like him a lot

SEX and the pregnant girl
(*Cosmopolitan*, November, 1993)

What we love about men's bodies!
(*Cosmopolitan*, September, 1993)

High Impact, Low Emotion: Why men like SEX with strangers!
(*Cosmopolitan*, May, 1993)

Will you see him coming?
How to pick a man who's very, very good for you

What's the ultimate male fantasy? No, not *that* one!
(*Cosmopolitan*, March, 1993)

Should you have sex with your ex-lover? (Probably not, but we all do!)

Where are the men for successful women?

The best is yet to come!
What's great at 18, thrilling at 25, sensational after 30? SEX SEX SEX!
(*Cosmopolitan*, June, 1993)

Selling sex on the cover ain't recent. The cover of March, 1968's *19* asked 'WHERE HAVE ALL THE VIRGINS GONE?' On the subscription page, where *Cosmopolitan* advertizes its subscription rates, there is a 'statement of intent'. That is, a *Cosmo* manifesto:

> *Cosmopolitan* is dedicated to helping young women in every area of their lives, but the heart and soul of *Cosmo* has always been relationships. We take you through the minefield of sex with warmth and humour...Want to know what makes men cheat? What keeps them faithful? 101 uses of sex? It's all between our covers. Turn to *Cosmo*, too, if you want a career as opposed to a job, if you want to keep fit and look terrific, if you want to know how to entertain at home with flair.[36]

Here what it regards as most important to its *raison d'être*: 'relationships', i.e., young, bourgeois, white, First World, affluent and heterosexual relationships.

Getting the balance right is part of the editor's job. As the editor of *Cosmopolitan* put it in 1983, for example 'one sex article and six emotional articles, and one a negative and one a positive article' (J. Winship, 1987, 100). The typical *Cosmo* article begins by setting out a problem, bringing in various 'experts' to discuss it, also using the author's own friends and experience, finally offering up some advice and morals. Typical articles on that all-important *Cosmo* word, 'relationships', included "Licensing your live-in lover" (November, 1983), "Is marriage dead?" (June, 1981), "Pillow friends" (September, 1978) and "Sex and the single parent" (August, 1981). Typical *Cosmo* sex articles included: "Sexual commitment: can it satisfy?" (September, 1983), "What next for sex?" (March, 1982), "Your most personal sexual experience" (November, 1983), "Skin to skin: clothing the erogenous zone" (October, 1983) and "A little more than breakfast in bed" (July, 1982).

Another *Cosmopolitan* article on relationships suggests there are seven 'stages of a relationship': Euphoria, Fantasy, Discovery, Disillusion, Attunement, Splice and Split.[37] Each stage is illustrated with photographs of celebrity couples. Kate Moss and Johnny Depp, supermodel and movie brat, illustrate the 'euphoria' stage, staring into each other's eyes. Farah Fawcett and Ryan O'Neal illustrate 'love gone sour' ('disillusion'). Paul

---

36 "Subscribe to *Cosmopolitan*", *Cosmopolitan,* May 1994, 218
37 Naomi Miller: "The Seven Stages of a Relationship", *Cosmopolitan,* October 1994, 184-7

Newman and Joanna Woodward depict 'splice' (marriage).

Here, the link is graphically and colourfully made between love and fame, between the love lives of celebrities and the love lives of the readers. The readers' lives are illustrated by the celebrities. It's an æsthetics of love in which the cultural exemplars are culled from mass, popular media. Like advertizing, 'women's magazines' appropriate pop and movie stars for their own ends, fusing their readers with the glamour of celebrities. The reader is encouraged to identify her/ his life with that of the pop or movie star. In the throes of early love, the reader sees the fashion supermodel cavorting with the movie stud, and thinks, *yes, that's me too.* After all, this is how all the media, and all art, works. Personal identification is the foundation on which all media and art operates. Without personal identification, nothing can work.

July, 1994's *Cosmopolitan* has all the usual ingredients, this time given a 'summery' feel: the photographs that accompany the features are of women on beaches, with men on beaches, lolling around in swimsuits. There is a feature, a double-page spread, called "Why you should make love tonight: a large (two-page) colour photo of a topless young woman in jeans lies in the surf, her jeans wet, leaning back and kissing a topless young man. Surrounding the blissful, holidaying heterosexual couple are short sentences in white type:

'There's nothing good on TV',
'The afterglow leaves your skin firmer and younger looking',
'Because he's there',
'Your frantic gaspings at the peak of passion won't damage the ozone layer',
'An orgasm is the best stress-buster we know'[38]

Here sex is regarded as good for the ecology! (ozone layer), for your looks, for your health, for your relationship ('Because he's there'). *Cosmo* clone *New Woman*'s article "50 reasons to have sex" includes:

No. 3. Because it's a working day. You haven't really got time. (But what the hell!)

[38] *Cosmopolitan*, July 1994, 162-3

No. 25. Because you're a grown-up now. In other words, because you can![39]

There are articles in July, 1994 *Cosmopolitan* on "15 things you should know about feet"; "Love changes" (Hollywood's broken romances, complete with large colour photos – Mia Farrow breaking up with Woody Allen, Liz Taylor and John Warner, Brigitte Nielsen and Sylvester Stallone, Isabella Rossellini and Martin Scorsese, etc, another trawl through the world of media celebrity); "Men's things" (men and their possessions, such as record collections, cars, mobile phones, here termed 'penis extensions' – the article is illustrated by a photo montage of a carphone sticking out of a nude man's groin, in place of a pecker); "Ex directory: sex and the single girl" (a piece on the lure of ex-lovers: 'why do I keep phoning yesterday's men?'); articles on career, offices, being fired, "Make it in marketing"; and the perennial 'relationships' articles, articles on bourgeois heterosexuality: "When he decides it's over"; "3 years on"; "Not everyone should have a child"; more idiot images of women in another article, "Hollywood thighs", a montage of images of movie stars' thighs (Sophia Loren, Daryl Hannah, Raquel Welch, etc).

---

39 Mark Edwards: "50 reasons to have sex", *New Woman*, June 1994, 76-77

"SEX SEX SEX!"

'SEX SEX SEX!' *Cosmo*, famously obsessed with sex, which defines sex as central to heterosexual relationships, states: '[s]ex can be magic'.[40] *New Woman* (April, 1994) has an article on Betty Dodson, a '65-year-old American sex guru', who teaches women about sexuality, how to masturbate, have good orgasms, etc.[41] Rare are the anti-sex or asexual voices in 'women's magazines'. True, there are pieces on impotence or people who have physical or psychological problems with sex,[42] but rare is the feature on people who are simply not interested. It is assumed by the authors of 'women's magazines' that it's OK to go without sex for a while, but *forever*? No way. 'Fran, age 26' in *Cosmopolitan*, says:

> I don't believe the stories I read of women having a marvellous sexual time, describing their fantasies, not reality.[43]

All the glossy monthly 'women's magazines' use sex to sell copies. 'YES, WE'RE LIVING IN SIN | NO, WE'RE NOT GETTING MARRIED | WHY? IT'S OUT OF DATE' ran the cover-line on a *Nova* cover (in March, 1967), next to a picture of a young white couple and a child. One issue of *More!* has the cover-lines 'MEN WHO SAY NO TO NOOKIE!', 'ASTRO-SEX DATING' and 'SEX WITH A MALE FRIEND'. In the 1980s and 1990s the monthly agony column not only became more and more concerned with sexual matters, it spread to other magazines. Magazines aimed at men took up the sex 'n' emotions agony column (*GQ, Arena, Loaded, Sky*).[44]

For some critics, it's a mystery why women readers should be interested in how to have fifteen orgasms in a night. For the bemused critic, 'women's magazines' such as *Cosmopolitan* and *Marie Claire* offer a 'fantasy world'

---

40 Alice Kosner, *Cosmopolitan* August 1985, 128
41 Annie Savoy: "This woman masturbates for a living", *New Woman*, April 1994, 70-72
42 For example, *She* has a 'malfunction of the month' slot, "Anorgasmia", *She,* March 1986, 117
43 Carol Lee: "Why women are still waiting for the sexual revolution", *Cosmopolitan*, December 1984, 128
44 Ellie Hughes: "Do they really mean us?", *The Independent on Sunday*, 3 September 1995, 11

– the amazing sex life, the wonderful career, the loving husband/ partner, the gorgeous body. One male broadsheet critic asks '[d]o women really want to read this sort of rubbish? Surely, they are more interested in the art of gracious living than the secrets of the G-spot?'[45] Another broadsheet critic (Neal Ascherson) found that the articles on sex the glossy 'women's magazines' advertized in bright, chunky typography ('Illicit Sex' (*Marie Claire*), 'Hotter Than Ever Sex' (*Cosmopolitan*), 'The Best Sex I Ever Had', (*Company*)), turned out to be often hopelessly idealistic. Beneath the 'raunchy titles in red, yellow and black across the glossy covers' were articles by 'that half-forgotten generation of feminists and idealists who had faith in women, who had hope in sex as a sacrament'. Ascheron's wry, disbelieving newspaper column concludes that

> all the pornish fanfares conceal the same valiant, indomitably hopeful debates about how to handle emotions and how to humanise men which have preoccupied women for the last hundred years.[46]

SEX SURVEYS

Cosmopolitan does surveys. They are one of the delights of 'women's magazines'. *Cosmo*'s quizzes, about sex, included July, 1972's "Are you really permissive?" and August, 1974's "Are you sexually adventurous?" Sex surveys often throw out conflicting data. If people tend to lie in political surveys, they are even more likely to lie about intimate, anxious matters such as sexuality. For example, in a 1993 Janus survey 83% said their marriages were good or great. In the same year, though, *Cosmopolitan* found that 50% of married men cheat on their partners. In 1994 a survey

45 Cosmo Landesman: "Baring all in a model industry", *Sunday Times*, 15 October 1995
46 Neal Ascherson: "We can have enough sex but never enough sexual gossip", *The Independent on Sunday*, 15 October 1995

for *Cosmopolitan* rival *New Woman* reported that 75 per cent of women did not believe in marriage any longer.[47]

In *Cosmo*'s May, 1994 issue, there is "The *Cosmo* Relationship Survey":

Is it important for you to have someone special in your life, or are you happy with being single? Do you think marriage still has a place in our society or would you prefer to live with someone? Do you need a partner at all? And what about sex? Do you make love often or only now and again?[48]

Questions in this *Cosmopolitan* 'relationship survey include:

No. 4. Which of the following (if any) do you dislike?

1. Kissing on the mouth
2. Having your breasts fondled/ kissed.
3. Your partner masturbating you.
4. You masturbating your partner.
5. Receiving oral sex.
6. Giving oral sex.
7. Anal sex.

Each question has multiple choices, Often in questionnaires, the people surveyed reply, 'well, my answer's not really any of those answers'. When pushed, they might reply, 'well, my answer's closest to B.'

No. 26. Which of you thinks sex is more important?

1. You.
2. Him.
3. You both think it's equally important.

Probably the most interesting question in the *Cosmo* survey is this, where a list of factors in a 'good relationship' is given:

No. 52. What do you think *women* want from their relationships? (Rate in order of importance, I being the most important.)

47 Nick Cohen: "Lies, damn lies and sex surveys", *The Independent on Sunday*, 21 January 1995, 6
48 "The *Cosmo* Relationships Survey", *Cosmopolitan*, May 1994, 37

1. Love.
2. Fidelity.
3. Companionship.
4. Sex.
5. Children.
6. Financial security.
7. To look after someone
8. To have someone look after you.
9. Fun.
10. Emotional Support
11. To be part of a "team"

The next question is equally telling. It has the same list of answers as above, but the questions is:

What do you think *men* want from their relationships?

A survey in October, 1994's *Cosmopolitan* showed that three quarters of *Cosmopolitan*'s audience (or three quarters of the women who responded to the survey) were in their 20s, mostly between 19 and 24.[49] This survey confronts the issue of *Cosmopolitan* being sex-obsessed. It says:

> "Why do you have so many articles on sex?" is a cry we hear often at *Cosmo*. But when we asked how you learned about sex, magazines (19%) proved to be a bigger source of knowledge than school (11%), parents (13%) or your first lover (18%). (p. 26)

Cosmopolitan, then, sees itself having an educational role. It has a mission to teach about sexuality, health, beauty, lifestyle, travel, and the all-important 'relationship'. It is this mission to teach that sometimes comes across as zealous and evangelical.

British broadsheet newspapers also run sex surveys, and sometimes present them (as *The Independent* did) in a similar way to 'women's magazines' (illustrations, graphs, and quotes from 'real' people defined as 'Martin, 31' or 'Suzanne, 27'). In *The Independent*'s 1996 survey typical results included: a lot of people (46%) who disproved of adultery, S/M

---

49 Elaine Robertson: "Relationships Now', *Cosmopolitan*, October 1994, 26

(45%), anal sex (43%) and gay sex (40%).[50]

In the *Cosmopolitan* survey, we are told that '[a]lmost half (49%) of you would like to have sex more often' (29), '[t]wo out of 3 respondents are in a sexual relationship' (29). The lists of 'qualities' which the survey wishes to ask the reader about are enlightening:

How do you rate the qualities that make for a successful relationship?

1. Shared sense of humour
2. Common interests
3. Wanting the same things in life
4. Good sex
5. Fidelity

The list goes on to mention thirteen qualities in total.[51] More questions in the survey include:

What do you think women want from their relationships?

1. Love
2. Companionship
3. Fidelity
4. Fun
5. Emotional support
6. Sex

What do you think men want from their relationships?

1. Sex
2. Love
3. Companionship
4. Fun
5. To have someone to look after them
6. Fidelity[52]

What these questions simplistically but graphically illustrate in the world of magazines are the conflicts in goals between men and women. They

---

50 Hester Lacey: "A chorus of disapproval", *The Independent on Sunday*, 21 January 1995, 6
51 Elaine Robertson, op. cit., 30
52 Robertson, op.cit., 32

show, albeit in a *very* simplified way, the differences between what women value in a relationship, and what men value. Women say they want, first, love, then companionship, fidelity, fun, emotional support and sex. According to the *Cosmo* survey, women value love, companionship, fidelity, fun and emotional support above sex. Meanwhile, women reckon that what men want from a relationship above all is sex, followed by love, companionship, fun, someone to look after them and fidelity. According to the survey, women value love and faithfulness much higher than men. Also telling is that the top three entries for women's desires in a relationship are love, sex and fidelity, while women reckon men want sex, love and companionship, fidelity rating at number six.

Cosmopolitan's women readers, it seems, do not have many illusions about what men are after. 'Men are just after one thing' (sex) is an old wives' sort of maxim. However, if we have to sum up men's desires in a single word, it would be more accurate to say that masculinity or patriarchy is after *power*. Or *control*. For, when you have power, all your wishes are granted. You are the baby emperor, commanding a genie to grant your every wish, whether it be for blowjobs, drugs, fast cars or fame. *Cosmopolitan*'s readers acknowledge that men are hungry for sex, and in doing so they also acknowledge their role in the politics of a heterosexual relationship (as sexual providers, as sexually desirable). Both men and women put 'fun' at number four, but at number five women put 'emotional support', while men are seen as desiring not so much 'emotional support' as someone to mother them: 'to have someone look after them'.

It's a commonplace notion that men are sometimes neurotic about their own sexualities, and this worry often centres around their penises. Penis size is a theme that crops up in teen magazines, for boys and girls (*is is big enough? is is too big? is it the right shape?*), in pornography (*God, it's so big!* a zillion women sigh in porn mags and videos), and in many 'women's magazines'. The back of magazines of general interest, in the classified sections of newspapers and in the free weekly ad-papers, there are adverts such as this:

IMPOTENT?

NOT ANYMORE thanks to the House of Pan PENIS DEVELOPER *GUARANTEED* to work through VACUUM FORCED INFLATION *O R YOUR MONEY BACK* [...] Return ad with order for a spare FREE PUMP

•

An operation to increase both **LENGTH AND GIRTH OF THE MALE ORGAN** is performed in London & Northern venues by a fully qualified **HARLEY STREET SURGEON** experienced in this field.[53]

The flipside of the classified sections of 'women's magazines', with their cosmetic surgery, liposuction, health and beauty adverts, are the ads for penis extensions, penis lengthening surgery and the like. Worries about dick size often crop up in agony columns (*my boyfriend's penis is too small* might be a worried remark from a letter writer – or, more typically: *my boyfriend's worried about the size of his penis*). We are used to men being obsessed with their penises at times, but *Cosmopolitan* is too: it is a question that often appears in *Cosmo* questionnaires. Having a big dick is a status symbol for men, like having a 'tight butt' or prominent breasts for a woman. The large schlong is an object of reverence among men (and women). It makes men stand out in the group situation, among peers (in the shower). Men with large penises are regarded with awe in the media and among pea-brained punters: the large penis is a badge of status among rock stars, for example (Jimi Hendrix, Mick Jagger, Robert Plant). It's the same for other male heroes and icons (footballers, porn stars, movie stars, athletes). The large weener becomes a key component of some celebrity's status, just as, for women, large breasts are sometimes seen as a crucial element in their stardom (Marilyn Monroe, Raquel Welch, Dolly Parton).

---

53 in *The Guardian*, 19 August 1995

LIFESTYLE

WHEN 'women's magazines' began to decline in circulation through the 1970s and 1980s, this may have been due in part to the new material about rape and other 'hard' items. The German magazines, *Bella, Best* and *Take a Break* came onto the magazine scene with TLS (true life stories) and TOT (triumph over tragedy) stories. Accessibility was the key, and sales grew.[54] Populist 'women's magazines' have always over-simplified matters. In some 'women's magazines', 'this month's sexual position' is featured: a splurge on a 'sexual position' the reader can try with her/ his partner each month. Next to a drawing of a man lying on top of a woman, both of them face-down, is the line: 'this position may seem a little impersonal'.

'Women's magazines' assume the reader knows utterly nothing, and so are always educating their audience from the basics upwards. 'Women's magazines', like all magazines, always start form the foundation upwards. They assume their audience consists of first-time readers and first-timers to a particular subject. Thus, a feature on 'how to make the boys go wow!' will always begin by setting out basic, simple premises. An exploration of violence in the home will often begin with basic facts, a lead-in to statistics and social workers' opinions. Thus, magazine articles always spend much time 'educating' the reader. This means that magazine articles, like all aspects of the media, never get very far. They are always wading through the basics. Development and sophistication becomes harder and harder to achieve, because one is always trawling through things one already knows. Magazines offer a lot of text about a lot of subjects, but not in any great *depth*. It's the same with television and radio: a plethora of texts, but with little real substance to them. Viewers know they can switch on a TV programme and 'get' it within a few seconds. Watch five minutes and you 'get' the whole show. It's the same with magazines and newspapers: read a few lines and you catch the whole piece.

It's as if people want to be told the same thing over and over again. As if they need to hear the same thing time after time.

---

54 Peter Cole: "Bad news for the safari-suit brigade", *The Sunday Times*, 21 November 1993, 4, 6

This superficiality is not all bad, of course. It's often very useful to have the basic facts on a subject set out again. But this aspect of the media, found everywhere, leaves less and less room for the deep and detailed development of issues. The more time you spend introducing people to the fundamentals of a subject – Imperialism, say, or contraception – the less time you have for exploring the finer points, the more ambiguous aspects of the subject. The emphasis on keeping articles to 2500 words, the pressure to deliver 1000 words on geopolitics by tomorrow, forces the print media to over-simplify, to summarize subjects too quickly, missing out other points of view. The journalist, naturally, falls back on her/ his own experience, or (often limited) views of events, so that, even in seemingly 'objective' reports, subjectivity is at a premium. For the very ratio of number of words to the topic under consideration forces the more unusual, the more anguished or bitter or confused or difficult viewpoints to be excluded.

The print media, then, 'flattens' subjects continually, in an effort to 'cover' the whole subject in a limited space and time. It's the same in radio and TV, both time-dominated media. While in some of the more academic or smaller journals one finds longer, more 'in-depth' articles, these are not found in the populist media. Each article in 'women's magazines', as in most populist media, can be consumed in three or four minutes. The domestic/ home-based. more 'traditional' women's magazines, such as *Take a Break, Bella* and *Woman's Weekly*, provide a host of very short items, each of which can be consumed over a two minute coffee break, or on the bus between stops, while the broadsheet newspapers often print a soft news story at the base of the front page, that can be read with the paper folded up, as one sways to and fro on the commuter train, or staggers homeward. The idea, as with TV ads or news soundbites, is the quick and easy digest of information, of information as snack food: the food you can eat between meals without ruining your appetite, as they used to say of *Milky Way* chocolate bar.

The features in *Cosmo* are not *all* about sex, but most of them do revolve around the notion of sexually active single women, and sexually active women in relationships. Marriage and weddings, babies and parenthood are not featured in *Cosmo* (although pregnancy test kits are advertized). Rather, the '*Cosmo* woman' is in control of her life, working full time, living in her own apartment in some urban area, with one or two 'serious'/ long-term relationships under her belt ('[y]ou're aiming high! *Cosmo* readers are ambitious, well-educated and career-minded', questionnaire, April, 1982).

Other features in *Cosmopolitan* relate to heterosexual relationships: "Sex in the Movies", a look at the portrayal of eroticism in cinema, i.e., Hollywood notions of sex; "The politics of muscle", an extract from Gloria Steinem's book;[55] "Call me irresponsible", a piece on being 'unreliable'; a 'News Report' on male violence; "Are you ill or is it hypochondria?"; and so on. September, 1993 offers on its front cover the following features: 'Big growth areas: fellatio on the upswing, male multiple orgasms and other SEX findings for you to chew over', 'The world's most delicious lesbian on love, SEX and men', 'Tender is the night: What makes the famous fall in love?', 'What we love about men's bodies', while the July, 1994 *Cosmo* cover includes: 'Can your relationship pass the three-year test?', 'What makes a man decide the affair is over?', 'The sexiest bikinis' and 'Why you should have sex tonight'.

> *Cosmo* always assumes its readers are part of a heterosexual couple, or aspiring to be; whatever the text says, there's no mistaking the images. The 'new woman' *Cosmo* version is the sexy woman. Sex equals not only fun, but independence and success.[56]

The ads in 'women's magazines' back this up: ads for railway trains (in Britain, the Intercity company) depict a bourgeois couple having a lovely, smiling time on a train ('In cars, romance is quite elusive,/ The train however, is most conducive' runs the copy).[57] While a train journey may be 'romantic' (after all, one of the most 'romantic' of British films - in the eyes of movie buffs - the ultra-insipid *Brief Encounter*, occurred in and around

55 Gloria Steinem: *Moving Beyond Words*, Bloomsbury 1994
56 Janet Lee: "Care to join me in an Upwardly Mobile Tango? Postmodernism and the 'New Woman'", in L. Gamman, 168
57 Intercity advert, in *She*, April 1994, 38

trains), it's difficult to find items as mundane as toothpaste romantic. Yet advertizers continually employ romance to sell products: so we find, above a photo of a tube of 'Rembrandt Whitening Toothpaste' a photo of a smiling, clean, bourgeois couple. The colours of the ad – the black, stylish clothes and the golden, glowing faces – suggest elegance, togetherness, love embodied by smiling faces, with perfect white teeth ('I love to see your smiling face' is the copy line, presumably the man whispers it the woman).

Cosmopolitan has pages and pages of fashion and beauty: ideas for what to wear, how to look beautiful, how to improve your skin, your hormone balance, how to get fit, etc. There are reviews, or rather, highly compressed (i.e., very short) *pre*views of books, films, TV, music. There are advice and 'tips' columns on money, travel, career, and food. There is the agony column, always one of the most popular parts of any 'women's magazine' ('I am 16 and have an 18 year-old boyfriend who wants to have sex...,' 'I am 18. My girlfriend is 15. We are both virgins. I want to have sex...', 'My problem is girls – they won't go out with me').[58] The agony column is 'actuality' media, talk about talk about real stuff, where the discourse of sex and intimacy is thrust into the foreground, where the agony aunt often recommends 'have you tried talking about it?'[59] There is the short story, and all manner of offers and adverts.

In sum, *Cosmopolitan* offers a good deal of information, like most magazines. But *Cosmopolitan*, like all magazines, endlessly recycles material. Thus, most of the features and fashion and beauty and editorial matter is rehashed from earlier work. Most of the articles could be put into any other month of the year, or the decade. Thus, a feature on 'why he doesn't love you anymore' or 'what to do about eyebags' could appear in the Christmas issue, the April issue, or the September issue. What changes in the features, from time to time, is the graphics, and the photos that accompany each feature. Thus, 'when your best friend steals your man' can appear as a flowery, summery feature when accompanied in the July issue

58 Kathy Myers: "Understanding advertisers", in Howard Davis, 1983, 211
59 Rosalind Coward: "Have You Tried Talking About It?", *Female Desire*, Paladin 1984; Shelagh Young: "Family Affairs: Angst in the Age of Mechanical Reproduction", in Day, 1990, 112

by a photo of three people on a beach: two women, one man, you've seen
it a million times before: the man and the best friend' are whispering and
grinning about love, while the second woman stands apart, frowning. The
second woman is you, and you are watching your best friend take your
man. Alternatively, for the October, the picture editor selects a similar
photo, but set on an urban street with gloves and scarves and Autumnal
colours. Easy.

Self-improvement is one of *Cosmo*'s watchwords: 'Learn a language this
summer', 'Change your face in a day', 'Work off that extra weight'. *Cosmo*
says you *should* be doing something, you *ought* to be doing this or that.
You *should* take that spur-of-the-moment weekend in Paris with your
clean-cut, affluent, blue-eyed, intellectual hunk, you *ought* to learn Spanish
tonight, eh? And while you're at it, why not improve the shape of your ass?

Cosmopolitan produces endless lists – of tasks, of things to do, places to
go, items to buy. Want to laze around by the pool sipping Martini and
scoffing chocs? According to *Cosmopolitan*'s ethics, you can only relax *if
you've earned it*. The '*Cosmo* woman' is no slob: she is very active, always
busy, with a diary bulging with appointments, people to see, things to do.
The '*Cosmo* woman's' day involves, typically:

¶ a light breakfast (fruit juice, slimming cereal)

¶ fitness work-out

¶ taxi to work

¶ hours of hard work, typically in management (*Cosmo* woman is often
shown sitting at a desk, holding a telephone, with a full diary before her)

¶ business/ power lunch somewhere swish

¶ working late; taxi again

¶ out in the evening to the cinema/ restaurant/ adulterous appointment

¶ lengthy make-down with the unguents and potions advertized in
Cosmo's pages, jacuzzi or hot tub

¶ fall asleep listening to a self-help or language tape

Cosmopolitan, like *She, Options, 19, Looks, Company, More!* and *Honey*, emphasizes zest, pizzazz, self-production and self-empowerment. By changing your lipstick, clothes, shape, style, attitude, you can change your life (A. Beezer, 107). The emphasis in *Cosmopolitan* is on 'being yourself', on self-actualization. But 'being yourself' means you have to be a lot of other things as well (great lover, great friend, great traveller, great cook, great stylist, great body, great humourist, great actress, great talent). *Cosmopolitan* is part of the personal change from domesticity to marriage to 'self-creation', as identified by Marjorie Ferguson (1983). The emphasis on the individual ignores people working in groups, such as in offices or factories: social power is seen as graspable by the individual (J. Winship, 1987, 120).

ADVERTIZING IN 'WOMEN'S MAGAZINES'

SOME (many) adverts are really quite astonishing. They present unbelievably bold representations, that nevertheless contain multiple readings, confusions and ambiguities. The ad for the Whirlpool 'super-fast cleaning hob', for instance, sets, like most ads, the banality of a commodity against visceral fantasy. The hob itself is placed low on the full page of a populist magazine. We see the flattened red circle of the electrical ring. So far all well and good: we see the object being advertized, a kitchen device, and a few lines of copy using the usual superlatives of advertizing: the hob, we're told is 'much faster', 'easy-clean', 'simple and safe'. 'heats in an instant', 'cleans in a flash', and so on.[60] The language of the Whirlpool hob ad is that

---

[60] The company name, Whirlpool, appears over a line that reads 'brings quality to life'. This is an unusual philosophical statement: that 'Whirlpool brings quality to life', as if 'quality' needs 'bringing to life' at all. Isn't quality already alive? Surely 'quality' is an abstract thing, a 'writing-effect', an adjunct of language, that can't be brought to life. Advertizing, though, promises to rejuvenate life, to make wonderful what was horrible. It's also a double meaning: adding quality to (your) life.

of all advertizing: 'heats in an *instant*,' 'cleans in a *flash*'. The implication is of a sudden, extraordinary electrical event in this heating device. Like photographs, movies, meteorite strikes, or gunfire, this hob acts suddenly, instantly, accompanied by flashes.[61]

The language of the Whirlpool hob advert – *flash, instant, super-fast* – is reinforced but also made decidedly secondary by the central image of the ad, the most astonishing thing about it: a huge woman is floating above the electric hob, blowing fire out of her mouth at the red circle of the heated ring. She is dressed in billowing, flowing robes, in scarlet and orange colours. She has long, ginger/ brown hair streaming behind her. She is a late 20th century, fashionable version of a Pre-Raphaelite woman – the woman seen in the art of Edward Burns-Jones and Dante Gabriel Rossetti, with long dresses, long auburn hair and bone-white skin. At the jokey level, the implication is that Whirlpool hobs come complete with a soaring fire-spirit who will light up your hob. The ad is startling in its visionary power, for here 'high art' is being employed in the most banal of services, the selling of a commodity. The Whirlpool hob is a powerful example of how advertizing mobilizes the structures of 'high art', symbolism (orange flames set against blue sky), graphic art, and the poetry of superlatives and positive philosophy. It is sexist in its implications about the audience and what the audience does (women and housework here).

One of the final readings may be that the utter drudgery of housework will be made magical and exciting by acquiring a Whirlpool hob. In using the Whirlpool hob, the buyer (intended here to be a woman) will become a fiery, Pre-Raphaelite wraith, clad in flowing orange robes. One could go further with this reading of a single ad: it shows that, beneath the vapid surface of advertizing, lie assumptions, ideologies and symbolisms that go to the heart of Western culture. Rosalind Coward commented:

> So, even though we may be feminists, even though we would resist
> these definitions of women, even though we personally would never
> make such statements, we have been caught up in the meaning produced

---

61 The implication is that this hob will act like a poltergeist or a UFO or a wizard in one of those ads or movies in the Spielberg tradition: lots of smoke, lights, and roaring noises.

by the advert.[62]

In a similar vein, and equally bizarre, is an ad for Deep Fresh foam bath: in the foreground is the side of a bath, with sponge and taps; the bathwater, though, merges into the ocean, and a naked woman is shown diving into the sea, her long hair streaming behind her.[63] This erotic figure is the reader of the ad in a fantasy incarnation, diving nude into a sunset sea.

Fantasy —› money. Advertizing —› money.

All readers are consumers. Fantasy and romance sells commodities. There is nothing to do but go shopping.

Another ad: for Halo (in *Cosmopolitan*, June, 1994), a chocolate bar that has 'only 97 calories' in it. In other words, Halo is a chocolate bar that you can chomp without getting fat. Wait a minute, we've been here before. What's so unusual about the Halo chocolate bar ad is not the copy line ('You don't have to be a saint to have a halo') or the superlatives employed to sell the chocolate bar ('wickedly delicious'), but the photograph used across the whole page to illustrate the ad. The model is young, white, 'pretty', semi-naked, wearing a swimming costume/ top/ dress (all we see is her head and shoulders and arms). She is in some city, brightly lit by sunlight, and she holds the chocolate bar in her left hand. All is par for the course so far. But the young woman has put one finger over the penis of a cherub fountain, the sort of fountain that spouts water from its pecker. From time to time photographs appear in the kooky section of the media showing people (usually old aunties) staring at a pissing cherub. Here, though, in the Halo ad, the woman's finger over the penis causes the water to spray over the woman. She throws her head back, laughing, as she is drenched with water. One reading of the ad is of the usual food ad: food = happiness, eating chocolate = happiness. The signals are the usual ones of advertizing: young 'attractive' woman, sunlight, warm colours, and pleasure. The usual associations of chocolate and luxury/ sin are made: chocolate is lovely but fattening. Like cream cakes, stuffing yourself with

62 R. Coward: "Underneath we're all angry", *Time Out*, 567, 1980, 6-7
63 Deep Fresh, *Good Housekeeping*, July 1983

chocolate is 'naughty but nice', as one ad campaign put it. (Thus, Halo is described as 'wickedly delicious'). Much as adultery is portrayed in blockbuster novels, eating chocolate is sinful but delicious.

Another reading might see the photograph of the woman being sprayed with water as an equivalent of the come shot or money shot of porn, where, to show the 'ultimate' in desire and gratification, the woman is sprayed with the man's semen. The water spraying everywhere in the Halo ad is clearly orgasmic. Caught in the sunlight, the drops scatter over the photograph like the divine seed of some latter-day Zeus. A mythological reading of this everyday advert is not out of keeping, for the cherub in mythology is the consort and assistant of the Goddess Venus. In Greek mythology, and in mediæval love poetry, Eros, portrayed as a young boy, is Venus's messenger of love. He's the one who fires arrows at lovers. You see this imagery still on Valentine cards. In the Halo advert for a chocolate bar, the young boy/ Eros is in erotic colloquy with the Goddess Venus. There she is, a young city woman, nearly nude, being washed by the sperm of her young consort, the pissing fountain cherub.

Finding mythic imagery in advertizing is nothing new. After all, advertizing is only one of many forms of narrative in the media, and all forms of narrative can be related to mythology, often to the Greek pantheon of gods and goddesses. In an ad for Vaseline Intensive Care Overnight Moisture Treatment Body Cream, a woman lies asleep on a large white bed. Above her is a huge full moon, glowing. The moon is the prime symbol of the night, the unconscious, dreams, and all things occult, as well, of course, the symbol of menstruation. These connotations are appropriate, as the ad, in *Cosmopolitan* magazine, is aimed at young women. The implication is that, like the moon, Vaseline Intensive Care Overnight Moisture Treatment Body Cream will watch over you. It will keep you safe throughout the night. As you sleep, Vaseline Intensive Care Overnight Moisture Treatment Body Cream will be working. It will be your guardian angel.

Commodities have the powers of some of the gods. In a godless world, we don't have saviours or guardians, but we do have body creams and hoovers, I-Pods and cell phones, and toilet paper in a million different colours.

One of the most amusing aspects of *Cosmopolitan* is not intentional: the photographs that are printed to 'illustrate' or accompany the features. These photographs contain unnamed, anonymous individuals in various poses embodying some aspect of the article. Thus, next to 'power at work' we see a picture of a powerful woman, surrounded by three men, one with a mobile phone, another taking notes, the third talking to the woman. She is a business-woman, successful, and in control of a bevy of male assistants. Next to an article on business trips abroad, another anonymous photo shows a smart, smiling woman entering an upscale hotel. Next to "How he knows it's the real thing", a piece by one of the few male *Cosmo* contributors on how men 'just know' when they're in love, is a photo of a woman kneeling astride a man on a beach.

These photos can seem odd at times, for they are variations on the '*Cosmo* woman', the '*Cosmo* woman' in action: seen at business meetings, joking with friends, sitting on beds discussing make-up, having a romantic cappuccino with a man in some café, striding down the street with a clutch of designer bags, etc. The photos are interchangeable, and have remained the same, bar a few fashion changes, for years.

Another portrayal of the '*Cosmopolitan* woman' occurs in the US edition of *Cosmo* (from 1988). The ad in which this version of '*Cosmo* woman' appears is an ad for *Cosmopolitan* itself. That is, this ad appears in *Advertising Age*, a media mag, and is aimed at prospective advertizers, inviting them to advertize in *Cosmopolitan*. The woman is shot from the back, and above her head the *Cosmopolitan* cover page logo appears back to front. The tag line is 'the power behind the pretty face', suggesting the old notion of the get-ahead woman being not only 'pretty' but powerful. The '*Cosmo* woman' is holding a clutch of consumer items behind her back, indicating that this is what the '*Cosmo* woman' desires/ has/ buys. She holds make-up brushes (indicating her beauty conscientiousness); a Pan Am World air travel card and a Hertz Rent-a-Car card (she travels worldwide, probably to do with her job); a CD of Wolfgang Amadeus Mozart (her eclectic cultural tastes); a calculator (she keeps a sharp eye on her finances); American Express gold card (she's got money); motorbike helmet and diving mask (she's healthy and active).

These items constitute a picture of *'Cosmo* woman' as active, strong, career-oriented, sexy, good-looking and, crucially for the advertizers, relatively wealthy. When magazines sell their readers to advertizers they always emphasize the reader's *buying power.* Our readers are sharp, cool, ambitious, quirky, sexy, the magazines say, but, most of all, they've got dollars and will spend 'em. As American *Cosmopolitan* puts it in its copy that accompanies the photo of the woman holding all those consumer items:

> You [the advertizers] assume she likes to get around [sex is implied here well as travel; *'Cosmo* woman' is someone who has lots of sex, who 'gets' (sleeps) around]. To her, that means a new set of wheels [she'll convert her erotic desire into material purchases: she'll buy the largest personal investment apart from a house: a car]. You figure she likes to keep in shape [the *'Cosmo* woman' cover model here has a 'shapely' body – in fact, her buttocks and hips are accentuated by her tight dress]. She knows that includes exercising her mind [stimulating mind/ soul as well as body, i. e., this woman's not dumb, not just a tasty piece of ass, she has – wow! – a *mind* too]. The truth is, the Cosmo girl knows more, does more, *earns more, spends more* [my italics]. THAT'S POWER [i.e., the power to consume, to spend]. THAT'S THE COSMOPOLITAN GIRL [that's the reader/ consumer you, the advertizer, should be reaching].[64]

An ad for *Cosmopolitan* that appeared in *The New York Times* in 1984 depicts a young white middle-class woman glamorously dressed, looking at the viewer. She is another version of *'Cosmo* woman'. Underneath the photograph of the *'Cosmopolitan* woman' is the copy line: '[o]ne of my most satisfying relationships is with a magazine'.[65] What a telling line. The enshrinement of heterosexual relationships, so central to *Cosmopolitan,* is here extended to the reader's relationship with the magazine itself.

Another odd element in *Cosmopolitan* is the advertizing. Not the amount of it: there's a lot, though, in *Cosmo,* as in most magazines. The point is, as

64 *Cosmopolitan* ad, in *Advertising Age,* 7 November 1987
65 *The New York Times,* 17 September 1984

with television, you can't tell where the adverts end and the magazine's editorial material begins.[66] There is a continuity between ads and features that goes beyond the usual notion of including ads within a 'house style' for the magazine. *Cosmo* produces 'advertorials' in partnership with companies. There are 'advertizing promotions' which *Cosmopolitan* publishes which are strange hybrids of the *Cosmopolitan* style and the mainstream ad agencies and manufacturing companies. For instance, the ad/ feature for Bellino swimwear, Bergasol suncare and Pernod in *Cosmopolitan*, May, 1979, unites the three commodities in one shot of a young white heterosexual couple on a beach. The man kisses the woman on the neck; she leans back, smiling rapturously (*wow*, the photo evokes, *bourgeois heterosexual sex is so orgasmically wonderful!*). She is nearly naked, wearing one of Bellino's bikinis. Both models are bronzed, using Bergasol sun tan oil, and a bottle of Pernod is on a table in front of them. The copy tells us that the fashion crew flew courtesy of Air France, and that the hairstyle was 'by Kerry for Molton Brown'. Every aspect of the 'advertisement feature', then, is for selling something, whether a hairdresser, an airline, sun tan oil, alcohol or *Cosmopolitan* itself.

Another ad, for Kerastase haircare commodities, directly copies the Irma Kurtz agony column format. The ad is structured exactly like a problem page: the (anonymous) questions in bold type face, the answers set in roman text.[67] But the questions in the haircare ad all revolve around hair 'problems' (too oily, lank and greasy, too dry, too mousy, etc). The ad becomes an extension of the magazine's editorial content, and each feeds off the other. The ads in *Cosmo* have to extend the magazine style and make the reader clearly aware of their product while remaining consistent with the rest of the magazine. In the *Cosmo* 'advertorials', the ads simply become an extension of the editorials. For the editorials anyway contain not-so-subtle consumer ideas, such as, in an article about stress at work, the writer will cite a book that just happens to have come out recently on that very topic. Author, title, publisher and price will be cited, so that the

---

66 Raymond Williams wrote: '[i]t is often not easy to separate advertising from editorial material.' *Communications*, Penguin, 1962, 55
67 Kerstase ad, *Cosmopolitan*, March 1980

editorial articles in 'women's magazines' becomes adverts and pseudo-reviews for all sorts of commodities.

The design/ editorial/ advertizing team on magazines have to be careful, though, that these combinations of magazine and manufacturer do not look like simple selling. The magazine may not wish to 'offend' its readership by backing up advertizing campaigns. The merging of advertizing and editorial turns everything in the magazine into some kind of sale. 'All you have to be is you', says the ad in *Cosmo* for Clairborne perfume, adding 'be a free spirit and celebrate your individuality with Liz Clairborne's Signature Fragrance for women'. Happily advertizing glosses over paradoxes which might scupper their hard sell, for how can you be 'individual' when you're relying on a mass produced commodity? Surely, if everyone is buying that particular perfume, you can't be 'individual', but only one of ten thousand other women who've bought it?

In other areas of *Cosmopolitan*, advertizing is the main ingredient. Advertizing is inescapable in *Cosmopolitan*. It's impossible to ignore it. For instance, in the preview pages where they say 'February is a great month to...' and they list a series of activities one can enjoy during February, the whole thing is advertizing. The book review pages feature photos of the covers of the books, exactly like the colour catalogues of publishers and distributors.

But it's in the style and beauty and health and fashion pages where the central role of advertizing is at its most prominent. Little colour photos of commodities are spread around the page, coupled with short bursts of texts in coloured and bold type which unashamedly sell the products. These pages are like having a range of commodities spread out on a store counter for you. You've just popped into Boots, say, and the headily-perfumed store assistant lays out a range of products for you: eye shadow, lipstick, moisturizer, shampoo, lip balm, facial wash, nail polish remover, wax strips, dry skin relief, scented soap, conditioner. The consumerism of 'women's magazines', then, becomes continuous with the consumerism of shopping. As you flick through the health and beauty pages, unable to distinguish between ads and features except by a few pointers, you are also shopping. As you read magazines, you can be shopping. One is meant to consider: *mmm*, I might buy that item next time I'm in town. Or, that swimming costume might look good on me. It's not that advertizing is 'bad' or 'degrades' a publication, or that consumerism is tacky, it's that *Cosmopolitan* and 'women's magazines' seem to found their fundamental ethos on selling the reader commodities. Selling itself is simply a part of capitalism, but when it flows into everything – into serious articles on racism or violence at home, say – it somehow trivializes everything. So that everything boils down to making a few (billion) bucks. Is that all there is? we wonder. Just another book/ film/ show/ shampoo/ perfume to sell? As far as magazines, which're adjuncts or tools of global capitalism, are concerned: yes.

In an ad for Kenwood hi-fi, the copy line is 'DON'T LISTEN TO IT. LIVE IT', meaning, one supposes, don't simply 'listen' to the Kenwood hi-fi, but 'live' it.[68] That is, turn the world of music (art) into a world of reality (life). The copy line is one of those comforting phases, such as Coca Cola's 'Coke is it'. The photograph that accompanies the Kenwood hi-fi advert is a complete lifestyle image. It shows a dark and moody world, an interior of some trendy apartment in a city. The colours are muted and dark, echoing the look and intended atmosphere of the hi-fi itself. Hi-fi since the 1970s has become increasingly sleek and matt black, or sleek and silvery, with buttons hidden or painted black. Inside the apartment, we see the hi-fi stacked on a trendy ironwork table: CDs and magazines are spread on the table; art prints hang on the wall; lilies are set on the window sill; there is an American 1950s style fridge; an old electric fan; a mountain bike leaning up against the wall; and a young woman (white, natch), sitting doing nothing in the foreground; she is wearing leggings and a T-shirt; she is *Cosmo* woman, healthy, single, sexy.

The gender-specific nature of shopping is well known by advertizers and manufacturers. In a typical mail order catalogue of, say, 1,100 pages, over 350 pages will be women's clothes/ fashion, compared to 120 pages for men; much of the rest of the mail order catalogue will be taken up with goods aimed mainly at women: household furniture (200 pages), kitchen-

68 Kenwood, *Clothes Show* magazine, November 1992, 80-81

ware (150 pages); traditional 'men's goods' – hi-fi, video cameras, computers, DIY tools – are given 60 pages.[69]

When we reach the black and white classifieds, at the back of *Cosmopolitan*, we find a preponderance of ads for health and beauty treatments. The cosmetic surgery ads are the among the most depressing in the media. Great, yes, that the First World possesses the technology to be able to change the bone structure or modify the skin. But the *reasons* for having cosmetic surgery turn out to be culturally determined, that is, often determined not by personal wish but by the pressure of society to look a certain way. All societies produce a set of norms, to which everyone is expected to conform. An odd-looking nose (though trivial, compared to famine in Africa) can be seen to be outside some norm of beauty. The cosmetic surgery ads, though, trade on a very ambiguous and confused sense of 'beauty', in which the prevailing system of 'beauty' is that of patriarchy. The cosmetic ads proclaim: 'IMPROVE YOUR LOOKS AND YOUR CONFIDENCE!', 'PERMANENT FAT REMOVAL!', 'DOESN'T EVERYONE DESERVE THE RIGHT TO FEEL GOOD ABOUT THEMSELVES?'. Terrible to recount, but according to the hype in a cosmetic surgery ad, a 38 year-old woman, Cindy Jackson, confesses 'I spent the past 5 years and over £25,000 finding out the truth about cosmetic surgery the hard way.'[70] No one 'forces' people to have cosmetic surgery, so what does make them do it? You can have your 'unattractive' nose reshaped, your breasts enlarged, fat sucked out of you, moles and cysts removed, your eyebags removed, your ears 'corrected', your tummy tucked, and so on.

Why does a person think their body 'unattractive'? What is this notion, being 'attractive'? Does it mean merely pleasant to look at, or is sexual desire involved? Who decides what is 'attractive'? What are the criteria, laws, codes of 'beauty'? Do they apply to everyone, or just some people? Is beauty universal and unchanging, or is it, rather, affected by the pressures of race, age, status, class, politics, ideology, etc? Surely 'beauty', being 'relative', is *cultural*, that is, conditioned by so many factors (social,

---

69 *Burlington*, catalogue, Winter 1994/5
70 Cindy Jackson in The Cosmetic Surgery Network advert, *Cosmopolitan*, June 1994, 250

societal, psychological, symbolic, political, economic, ideological, ethnic, etc)? So when someone dislikes their nose or breasts their discontent comes partly from the external pressures of society. All this is obvious, it seems, but these external pressures come from a society in which there is more masculinism than feminism at work, in which the ideas, representations and ideologies favour patriarchal systems and masculinism. For some feminists, cosmetic surgery may be empowerment for women, where women take control of their bodies and change the way they look. For other feminists, cosmetic surgery may be an insidious and violent example of patriarchal systems in action, where women disfigure themselves in the name of the patriarchal norms, the patriarchal notions of 'beauty'.

In the advert for Nipplette ('[t]hrough gentle suction the Nipplette pulls the nipple out into a small, plastic, thimble-like cup'), which is a 'cosmetic' but not a 'surgical' process, we find the line '[e]mbarrassed by flat or inverted nipples?'[71] This line targets swiftly the emphasis on 'beauty' and the social pressures to 'look good'. This is the downside of consumerism, where one is made to feel bad about what one does not have. Great hair, great breasts, great hips, great finger nails, one must have them all. Thus, if you don't have a sports car/ mobile phone/ home/ laptop computer, adverts sometimes make you feel bad about it. Bourgeois Westerners are often surprised when someone doesn't have a car. *What, you don't have a car?* Or, *what, you haven't got a cell phone?* Or, *what? you ain't gotta computer?*

Cosmopolitan, and all 'women's magazines', stridently stress the importance of looks. For instance, 'women's magazines' print ads that emphasize the importance of looking good. The ads send out powerful signals about body-image, and its relation to consumerism. Whatever the cod feminism of the features in 'women's magazines' may say, the ads state the imperative of looking good and fashionable in no uncertain terms. Looking good means a 'shapely' figure, slim but rounded hips, pert breasts, no double chin, smooth, blemishless skin, hairless legs, etc. For the media,

---

71 Nipplette advert, *Cosmopolitan*, June 1994, 250

the handsome body is a social badge of success. Being successful is equated with looking good. 'The sleek, smooth, tight butt is a badge.'[72]

There are many aspects of the body to get right: hands, nails, feet, hips, thighs, waist, skin, hair, breasts, bone structure, mouth, eyes, genitals, etc. Have one of these elements of the body fail and the whole thing collapses. Look at the ads and fashion shoots in 'women's magazines' (or any magazines): they make sure no failures creep into the shot. It's no good having a model with smooth skin for a face shot if she's got an unsightly wart or a wonky eye. The body in 'women's magazines' is intensely scrutinized. It is ruthlessly dissected, and each body part is blown up – look at the huge close-ups of finger nails or women's lips in 'women's magazines'.

In 'women's magazines', feminism becomes 'depoliticized', as the features, editorials and adverts turn 'feminist *social* goals to individual lifestyles' (Rapp, 1988, 32), and personal 'lifestyle' becomes all-important. The (female) body becomes the site and centre of the cod feminism of 'women's magazines'. In 'women's magazines', feminism and 'femininity' merge in a 'commercial marriage' (Goldman, 1992, 133). Sexual freedom is equated with economic freedom, but both are only possible with a good looking body. The construction of a 'feminist' self in 'women's magazines' means the construction of a beautiful self-appearance. 'Women's magazines' imply that it is no good having a feminist revolution if it means women can't use a Braun Silk Epil Duo which offers 'super-smooth legs'. Feminism's no good if it means women have to wear dungarees, boots and no make-up. This seems to be a simplistic, trite interpretation of the feminism in 'women's magazines', until one really studies what the ads and fashion spreads are saying next to the 'feminism' of the editorials and features ('[t]here's a time and a place for everything – including being sexy' says a "Fashion is a feminist issue" article).[73] Feminism has been rewritten by 'women's magazines' and aligned to a voracious consumerism. In 'women's magazines', the language and imagery of feminism has been

---

72 Susan Douglas, "Flex appeal, buns of steel and the body in question", *In These Times*, 7-13, September, 1988, 19
73 Ellen Fairweather: "Fashion is a feminist issue", *Cosmopolitan*, July 1982

watered down and commercialized, a process that has been happening for decades – at least since the late 19th century (Cott, 1987, 172).

Looking good ('smart', 'cool', 'trendy', 'beautiful') is not, therefore, merely a matter of having other people admire you, or 'standing out' in a crowd. It is an economic imperative: a woman's 'beauty'-value is directly related to her economic 'value' in the labour market. Having the right face, the right body, car and possessions is a means to economic success. It is a way of constructing a social and personal identity, a way of maximizing one's value in the personal and public spheres, at home and at work. 'Being in control', such a key phrase in the quasi-feminism of 'women's magazines', means, in the terminology of 'women's magazines', being in control of one's life through one's acquisitions, one's career, one's social relationships, one's sexuality and one's own body. As an ad for Get Used jackets (in the US) put it: '[y]ou're sexual, but you control your choices.'[74] The idea is that the 'modern woman', 'today's woman', *Cosmo* woman', can 'control' all aspects of her life: further, she can perhaps 'control' the way she is perceived by others, by peers, bosses, relatives; she can perhaps, if she follows the right 'women's magazines', 'control' the mass of signifieds and meanings and connotations that surround her, so she can manipulate her self-image, the way she is 'objectified' by others. No one can push the 'modern would-be feminist woman' around, 'women's magazines' suggest, and the ads in them say it too: '[n]o one has the right to pressure you into anything that hurts your body, clouds your future, or robs you of your *self respect*' says a Lawman jeans ad.[75] Today's 'modern (*Cosmo*) woman' is 'independent', another key word, which indicates a free-thinking spirit capable of 'juggling' many aspects of her life, as *She* magazine puts it.

In fashion spreads, men often surround the model, often men who don't seem to pose any threat, such as old eccentrics like fishermen. In many fashion spreads, though, the man looking at the female model is clearly an admirer, a potential lover. One of the implications being that if you wear these clothes, you will be looked at, you with garner the *right kind* of

---

74 quoted in Goldman, 1992, 149
75 in *Mademoiselle*, September 1987

looks, that is, the look of admiration from someone you wish to impress. Fashion is all about trying to control how one is looked at, how to manipulate one's 'looked-at-ness'. A typical fashion spread all about controlling one's 'looked-at-ness' is "Pretty Woman", a series of fashion photographs in *Elle*, in which a near-topless woman (black bra and cardigan left open to show bra and chest) turns smiling to a (clothed) man behind her.[76]

Cosmopolitan, like all 'women's magazines', features many adverts that state, covertly, but often overtly, that looking good will make you feel good. And the means to this pleasure is heterosexual. In other words, by looking good, you will become attractive to men. It is so simplistic, so childish, one wonders how advertizers can imagine readers will buy such simplicity. Yet, in *Cosmopolitan* in 1994, we find the following advert: a full page colour photo of a woman (she is young, white, bourgeois, perfect skin, meticulous make-over, etc). She cocks her head to one side, her eyes sliding to the right, as if she's just glimpsed the obscure object of desire. The object of desire in this make-up ad turns out to be desirability, the ability to attract sexual partners, or, in the language of teen mags: BOYS BOYS BOYS. The copyline with this ad is: 'what difference does a tan make?', written in chunky capitals beneath the colour photo of the young woman.

On the next page, we find a photograph of the same young woman, now staring at the camera and grinning, sharing a joke with us. The joke? This time she is surrounded by four young men, four BOYS BOYS BOYS. The young woman, seen in a head and shoulders shot in the first photograph, was pale, in the second photograph she has a self-tan. At the bottom of the second page is the line 'FIND OUT FAST: Use 17's self-tan to get a safe, good-looking tan without sun'. The message is clear: get a tan and find out fast what difference it will make: it will make BOYS BOYS BOYS desire you. They will be crowding around you. Get the tan and you'll be the centre of attraction. Get the tan and BOYS BOYS BOYS will be after you.

The dominant message of this cosmetics ad is: self-tan = instant desirability. Advertizing has to dispel confusion and ambiguity, so this ad is

76 "Pretty Woman", photographer: J.R. Duran; fashion editor: Alisa Green; hair: Renato Campora for Atlantis; model: Joanna Rhodes, *Elle*, February 1993, 66

very clear about its message: the consumer is urged to 'find out fast' 'what difference a tan will make'. Every product offers (the possibility of) instant success. The 17 cosmetic ad structures success in terms of heterosexual desire, as does *Cosmopolitan* itself, as do all 'women's magazines'.

Another Boots No. 17 make-up print advert shows: first page: a young white couple, both white brown eyes and perfect skin, standing apart. Next page: the two are happy, both smiling, the woman being kissed by the man. The tag line in the first picture: 'wearing thin?' (i.e. make-up, but by appropriation, love also); on the next page: 'wear them thick'.

Another version of the Boots No. 17 make-up ad: head-shot, close-up, of a young woman, who's smiling, with blue water behind her. She is wet: copy line is: '[w]aterproof? Yes'. Next page, a shot of the same young woman, but being lifted up by a young man, both of them smiling, fooling around in the water. Copy line: '[b]oyproof? No'.[77] But make-up products themselves simply 'clog up the skin': what the cosmetics industry is selling is not a product but an 'image', an 'illusion', as a copy writer for a series of make-up product ads put it.[78] Make-up is 'feel good' stuff, a product designed to make people feel good about themselves.

Another Boots No. 17 advert, in *Elle*, shows a young woman (white, bourgeois, perfect skin) looking at the reader with a supercilious expression. The tag line: 'I'm covered in spots' (but the model, of course, isn't spotty on her face). Next page, the same young woman is surrounded by young men (white, bourgeois, perfect skin): the woman is wearing a spotty shirt and shorts, holding her arms over her head, in a display of her body, of her energy. The line is: '[w]anna count 'em'. The women is ventriloquized by the advert: she's saying to the men: 'wanna count my spots?', i.e., 'wanna look at me, study me, revere me?' The Boots No. 17 make-up ad is about female empowerment, about feeling powerful after the transformation the make-up will bring.

A Wolford tights ad shows a young woman (white, affluent, perfect skin, make-up) standing over two anonymous males dressed in black. Copy line: 'walk on the wild side... tights stay up body'. Implication: be wild with

---

77 Boots No. 17, *Cosmopolitan*, July, 1994, 117-119
78 In K. Myers, 1986, 76.

Wolford tights, be in control of two men, etc.[79] An ad for *Monsoon* perfume shows a couple (white, heterosexual, bourgeois) having sex. Well, we see their heads, eyes closed as if in orgasm, the woman on top of the man, holding his face to hers. Behind the sky, with thunder clouds and lightning bursting out, plus, of course, the pack-shot of the bottle of perfume. Connotations: orgasms like thunderstorms, the identification of the flood of juices at orgasm with the flood of rain during a monsoon. Use the perfume and you'll (possibly) have multi-orgasmic sex, sex like a monsoon. The tag-line is: '[u]nleash the power of nature.'[80]

In a Charnos lingerie/ sexy underwear ad in a 'women's magazine' a model, in five poses in five photographs, arranges herself to be looked at. She sits, looking down, demure, exactly like the Virgin Mary in countless Renaissance paintings. In other pictures she raises her arms or holds them apart, so the viewer can see her 'under-wired body with thong back', her 'basque, stockings and underwired bra'.[81] Another Charnos lingerie ad shows a white middle-class woman (young, perfect skin) reclining in a classic 'high art' nude pose (in the tradition of Jean Dominique Ingres, Titian, Correggio) in front of a painted backdrop of trees. She wears an 'underwired body'. The tag line is '[i]sn't it time the body you most admired was your own?' which puns on the meaning of the word 'body'.[82]

Go into a clothes store, and there is the music pounding, while a DJ tells you to buy buy buy, so you can look good. In the store and along the high street are posters and billboards expressing the need for good looks. On radio and TV, ads tell you that being 'attractive' is highly desirable. Pop songs preach the cult of 'beauty', as do Hollywood films, TV shows, newspapers. The cult of 'beauty' is partly about expectation: women are 'expected' to dress in certain ways. Men are too, of course, but men do not seem to have such an aggressive culture of fashion and appearances surrounding them and pressurizing them. Women complain about this, saying how wrong it is that women as they get older have to try to look younger, and after they reach a certain age, they become undesirable (or in

---

79 *Elle*, November 1992, 113
80 *Monsoon*, in *Company*, October 1994, 41
81 *Charnos* advert, *Company*, November 1994, 166-7
82 *Company*, November 1994, 102-3

Andrea Dworkin's terms, unfuckable). Men, rather, simply grow old and mature, grey and dignified.

BRA WARS

BRA ads show the double moral standards very clearly. A reaction to the 'supermodel' or 'waif' look of the late 1980s/ early 1990s was the 'fuller figure' fashion, epitomized by the 'curvaceous' bras, by Gossard and Playtex ('KNOCKS THE STUFFING OUT OF ORDINARY BRAS'). Bras seem to be made for men, who seemingly 'define' female fashion, and who love to ogle boobs. Yet, we return to this point time and time again, women judge their appearance in terms of what *other women* think, not men. Fashion seems to be patriarchal and driven by masculinist notions of what is 'beautiful' or erotic. Yet, if women are the primary source of opinions on fashion, then women are more deeply implicated in the patriarchal/ masculinist nature of the fashion culture than it seems at first.

Some bra adverts are indistinguishable from soft porn photos or the shots of semi-nude women bestriding the hoods of cars at motorshows. An ad for Berlei ('BE A BERLEI BEAUTY') shows two women posing like soft porn models, coyly but 'seductively' displaying their bodies for the viewer.[83] An ad for Wonderbra shows a woman (who is white, bourgeois, young) wearing nothing but a bra, staring at the camera. She is model Eva Herzigova, from the Czech Republic, who has a '36B superbosom'.[84] In an interview in *Looks* magazine, where Eva Herzigova is oh-so hilariously introduced "Cup hands, here comes Eva...', the model says 'I'm happy to show them off while they look pretty'.[85] The copy line is 'LOOK ME IN THE EYES AND TELL ME THAT YOU LOVE ME'. An alternative is: 'HELLO, BOYS!' and 'AND GOD CREATED WOMAN (ALMOST)'.

83 Berlei ad, *Cosmopolitan*, June 1983
84 Lisa O'Kelly: "I just, I just...I *just* improved my bust!", *The Observer*, 7 August 1994, 10
85 Sue Wheeler: "Wonder Woman", *Looks*, April 1994, 81

In another Wonderbra ad, in *Cosmopolitan*, Eva Herzigova stands looking at the viewer, topless except for the prominent bra. The copy line is 'MIND IF I BRING A COUPLE OF FRIENDS?'.[86] What are the model's 'two friends'? Why, her breasts of course. Another Wonderbra ad shows Herzigova smiling at the viewer, wearing a bra, her arms open to reveal her breasts. The opposite page says 'NOTICE ANYTHING DIFFERENT ABOUT ME?' The answer, not stated, but filled in by the reader, is: 'yes, you've got big boobs', or something like that. Underneath the main copy line is '[g]ot it in one'. That is, you've got the answer right to the question 'NOTICE ANYTHING DIFFERENT ABOUT ME?'

Another Gossard Wonderbra advert: a woman holds her hair above her head, smiling broadly. She is nude but for a black bra. The tag line is 'say goodbye to your feet'. That is, when you've got big boobs courtesy of Wonderbra, you no longer see your feet (or your nobbly knees, or protruding belly). Instead, you get loved.[87]

The downside of big breasts, artificially upholstered or otherwise, is small breasts. Here, bra manufacturers come to the rescue. There are bras for small-breasted women: '[n]ature may not have been overly generous with you, But Berlei have', proclaims an advert for Berlei bras. The text is set opposite a black-and-white photograph of a woman, smiling, clad in Berlei's bra and knickers. In large, curly, florid letters the tag line reads: '[m]y, how you've grown'. From 'little girl' to 'big girl', i.e., 'big-boobed girl'.

Wonderbra, 'the original push-up plunge bra', is portrayed, among other things, as an object of lust. Bras are designed for maximum cleavage. In the copy to bra ads, comfort is a definite second to having a great cleavage. It's an odd thing indeed that the sight of breasts lifted and squashed together should be so desirable. Women with big boobs are never taken seriously in the media, are always the object of ridicule (Diana Dors, Dolly Parton, Barbara Windsor, Pamela Anderson). Nipples are 'out of bounds' in mainstream 'family' entertainment (except in high fashion catwalk shots, some movies, 'high art', etc). Mainstream culture does not allow the

86 *Cosmopolitan,* December 1994, 92
87 in *Elle*, December 1992, 52

nipples to be seen, and many 'high fashion' designers ridicule this mini-taboo by drawing attention to the nipples by covering them up with a tiny piece of cloth. Pubic hair is even more 'taboo', so the cleavage is one of the prime signifiers of sexiness.

The bra adverts demonstrate in glamorous photos the ways in which you too can have a movie star cleavage. Some bra ads try the vamp approach (Gossard Ultrabra) with a woman made up with darkly defined eyebrows, red lipstick and the mouth lasciviously open. Some try the demure, 'feminine' look, with the model coyly smiling at the viewer (Triumph).

An infamous 'feminine' type bra ad was the Lovable ad which stated 'underneath they're [women're] all lovable'. For some feminists, this advert encouraged rape. That is, 'underneath they're all lovable' equals 'underneath they're all fuckable/ for fucking', in the terminology of feminists such as Andrea Dworkin and Mary Daly. Men, it seems, simply do not have to concern themselves with choosing this or that item of clothing to thrust their genitals forward or upward or have their balls squashed together to look appealing. There are items to 'enhance' male genitals, but these are a part of the pornography industry and S/M scene. Men are vainer than women, some claim, and concern themselves with hair, shaving, skin and fitness, but they are not usually expected to undergo having bits of their body squeezed together and exposed.

The Wonderbra ads received many complaints in Blighty, said the Advertising Standards Authority. A French ad for shower gel which briefly showed a woman's nipple garnered fifty complaints to the Independent Television Commission, 30 to the Broadcasting Standards Council and as many again to the individual ITV companies.[88] It's an odd thing the mere *sight* of bits of the human body should so offend people that they write or email or ring in to complain, odd when there are millions of people living in poverty worldwide, when thousands are kept in prison as political prisoners, and tortured, odd when there are millions of infinitely more important things to complain about than the sight of a breast. Why is it that men in particular get so worked up about a cleavage? It's something of a

---

88 Richard Brooks: "Censors get their knickers in a twist", *The Observer*, 15 May 1994

mystery, but good news for the manufacturers of underwear.

'Underwired', 'cotton rib', 'padded', 'front-fastening', 'stretch-straps' – the aim of these bras is always to 'enhance your bust', 'maximise your cleavage'. It's not 'lift and separate', in the old Playtex style, but knock 'em dead with a movie starlet cleavage.[89] 'Make the *most* of your cleavage' gushes Wonderbra ads. Put on the bra, and men will be forced to admit that they desire you. Put on the bra, and you'll have men falling at your feet, tongues lolling. You need never feel inadequate (size '32A') again. Here, wearing the Wonderbra/ Gossard/ Amourette/ Trousseau/ Autumn Leaf is not about feeling good in yourself, it's about feeling good because *you are desired*, feeling good because other people want you. This is what all adverts do: they suggest or try to persuade you that you will possess a desirable item if you buy the product. In possessing the desirable item, you in turn will become desirable. Get the new car and be the envy of your neighbours. Get the new conservatory and see 'em *drool*.

When the 'bra wars' between Gossard and Playtex were over, a new approach was tried out by the manufacturers and advertizers. The 'sports bra' became the thing, A Berlei sports bra advert showed a skipping rope 'shaped into a pair of pendulously sagging bosoms'.[90] The copyline was: 'If you don't wear a Berlei sports bra what shape will your breasts be in?' The idea was that, if you don't wear the Berlei sports bra you won't have a pert, desirous bust. Instead of the sexy vamp image of the Wonderbra adverts, the sportsbra traded on images of keeping fit and healthy – that is, not having a drooping bust.

89 Brigid McConville: *Mixed Messages: Our Breasts in Our Lives*, Penguin 1994
90 Hester Lacy: "It's new, it's scary, it's your bra", *The Independent on Sunday*, 17 September 1995, 10

3

FEMINISM IN *COSMOPOLITAN* AND 'WOMEN'S MAGAZINES'

THE boundaries between the feminist and non-feminist magazines is not clear (J. Winship (1987, 149). Fran Wheat, in *Spare Rib*, one of the more strident feminist magazines, said it was a pity there wasn't 'a halfway house between *Woman's Own* and the women's liberation publications'.[91] However, this is *Cosmo's* ideological ground, on the one hand enshrining traditional, patriarchal notions of 'femininity' ('*Cosmo* goes soppy over the wicked weekend', February, 1982); on the other, producing near-radical anti-porn diatribes. *Cosmopolitan* is marked from other 'women's magazines' by its self-confessed feminist agenda and aims. While some magazines suggest things for their readers to do or try, and while others recommend films or health ideas or 'good buys', *Cosmopolitan* i s particularly strident about its 'feminist' mission.[92] *Cosmopolitan*, unlike most other magazines, has a zealous mission to explain, and to preach. However, as we shall see, *Cosmopolitan's* feminism is extremely simplistic

---

91 Fran Wheat, *Spare Rib*, 134, September 1983
92 *Cosmopolitan* offshoot, *Zest*, in Autumn 1994, had features mainly on health issues (cosmetic surgery, 'the brain power diet', eating disorders, fashion and beauty)

and biologist, founded only loosely on Anglo-American feminist polemic.93

Despite its avocation of a politically vague feminism, *Cosmopolitan*, like *Vogue, Marie Claire, The Face, Bella, Sky, Slimming, Harpers & Queen, Looks, Just Seventeen* and *Empire*, presents an ideal form of 'woman' which is slim, attractive, smiling, self-confident and affluent. Readers of 'women's magazines' often complain that the models and supermodels in 'women's magazines' have unattainable bodies, impossibly thin and unreachably glamorous. It's not only sad that consumers think the perfect figures of fashion models are 'unattainable'. It's also sad that readers *desire* to be like them at all. Women, from before teenage onwards, often experience an immense pressure to look a certain way. This is what we might call 'the pornography of beauty', the fascism of fashion, where one becomes a 'fashion victim', like being a 'rape victim' or an 'anorexia victim' or a 'drug victim'. The 'pornography of beauty', which *Cosmopolitan* blatantly endorses, as do all 'women's magazines', as well all 'men's magazines', states that one must have, among other things: a perfect figure • slim hips • no flab around the belly • pert, non-sagging buttocks • long, manicured finger nails • shaved legs • a slender neck • no bags under the eyes • large, hypnotizing eyes • meticulously plucked eyebrows • gorgeous hair • full, pouting lips • no split ends • smooth, blemishless skin • no spots • no blotches • a slender nose • no pubic hair outside swimming costumes, and so on.

If one hasn't got these attributes, then 'women's magazines' suggest ways of achieving them. For instance, got a 'flat chest'? Simple: 'wear scarves, necklaces and shirts with breast pockets to add substance'; have you got a 'fat tum'? Easy: 'avoid any clothes that add bulk'.94 The readers/ consumers who express their wishes to 'look like a fashion model' make the mistake of confusing an *image* in a magazine with their actual flesh and blood self. The images in magazines are just that: *images*. The people look fabulous

93 The review section of October 1994's *Cosmo* quotes Andrea Dworkin a couple of times, in a short review of *Sexual Dating: The Official Politically Correct Guide* (Harper Collins, 1994): 'Intercourse: Before agreeing to or commencing intercourse, especially with a new partner, it's useful for a woman to pause for a moment and consider Andrea Dworkin's maxim: "Intercourse is the pure, sterile, formal expression of men's contempt for women."' (59)
94 Louise Pearce: "Stress the Best, Disguise the Rest", *She*, April 1994, 119 -120

for a number of reasons: firstly, photography can use any number of tricks to enhance 'beauty'; secondly, the images are mediated within the context of a magazine, accompanied by slick graphics, and printed on glossy paper; thirdly, the images are gushingly described in the copy, in terms identical with those in advertizing. But most importantly, the readers *desire* the images to be beautiful. Consumerism thrives on desire, and the consumer of magazines is filled with desire. If you stand back a little from the glamour of fashion magazines, you see the mechanics of manipulation. These images, though, are relentless, filling page after page, week by week, month by month. The cumulative effect is a constant flow of glamour and fashion. One can take it or leave it, but it's difficult not to be affected by it. Indeed, it would be impossible *not* to absorb one's environment and remain human in the accepted sense. And one's 'environment' is largely cultural, social, artistic. So all these images of 'beauty' and glamour and luxurious houses and 'beautiful people' must have an effect in promulgating the pornography of consumerism. Fashion is also, though, about controlling how one is looked at, about shaping the codes and messages of consumerism, about advertizing self-image to peers and strangers. Women sometimes speak of using make-up and clothes for themselves – not for other people, not their lovers – but for themselves.

The role models in the fashion magazines are obviously models and supermodels. Fashion models are held up as something to aspire to, and fashion models appear in many other 'women's magazines', not just the style and fashion mags. Time after time fashion models are the subject of features: what models do and think; what they wear; where they go; what they eat; how they make-over, etc. The latest round of waif-like supermodels (in the early 1990s) indicated the changing tastes in body size and shape, tastes which come and go continually. In the magazines, such as *Looks, Jackie* and *Just Seventeen*, women's body shape and size has to be validated by men: these magazines emphasize that it is the male/ masculine look that is the ultimate judge of female bodies.[95]

Sex sells perfumes: Jean Paul Gauthier's perfume comes in a bottle shaped like a woman, a headless, legless woman looking like a store

---

95 Sue Wheeler: "65% of men prefer curvy women", *Looks*, February 1994, 26-27

dummy, dressed in a basque with suspenders.[96] With over 700 perfumes on the market, you need all the gimmicks you can think of to sell your product: desire needs to be evoked to the maximum. The nude or sexual body does this job of arousal quickest. It's a competitive world. The fashion world is full of 'names' contending for the punter's attention, 'names' which include: Hamnett, Cerruti, Lacroix, Valentino, Christian Dior, Chanel, Versace, Hermes, Yves Saint Laurent, Karl Lagerfeld and Ungaro.

Sex sells: a double page advert in *Vogue* for gold shows a close-up of a woman's thigh, clad in black stockings and a dark blue velvet dress. The woman is pulling up her dress to reveal her thigh: the stocking is being held up by a gold fastener, complete with monogram. The tag line is '[s]ome legs are worth the suspense'.[97] The ad conjures up a darkly erotic world, in which the product (gold) is aligned with the promise of a sexual embrace not just by implication, but by the product actually appearing on the woman's body.

Magazines have to sell themselves to their advertizers: it is not simply a case of the advertizers coming to the magazine wishing to advertize in their pages. Magazines deliberately cultivate an environment which the advertizers will feel happy appearing in: *Cosmopolitan*, for instance, aims to 'create an image of the girl who reads [the] magazine' (Henkoff, 1979, 195), an image which the advertizers will not only be comfortable with, but will demonstrate a real ability to spend money on what the advertizers are offering.[98] (She is the 'Cosmo girl').

'Women's magazines' do not offer radical, uncompromising feminism. To do so would perhaps upset the consumerist equilibrium, and the all-important relationship magazines have with advertizers. You don't want to alienate sponsors and advertizers, so feminism in 'women's magazines' is

---

96 "Haute perfumerie", *Elle*, November 1993, 45
97 *Vogue*, October 1988, 63-64
98 Some of the advantages for advertizers in selling their products in 'women's magazines' include back reference, coupon response, image building, multiple exposure possibilities, precise targetting, complimentary environment and reaching TV viewers (B. Braithwaite, 121).

always toned down, always, like so much of the editorial content, a compromise. Writers have to write aware of the multi-layered pressures from editors, proprietors, advertizers, and society itself. In her article on *Woman* magazine, Janice Winship reckons that *Woman* offers a coherent view of femininity and feminism which is false.[99] In Winship's Althusserian approach, magazines such as *Woman* do not, and can not, challenge notions of 'femininity', for 'femininity' cannot be challenged from 'within'. For instance, the magazine can only engage with the issues raised on the problem page in its own terms (A. Beezer, 103).

Cosmopolitan, though it tackles 'issues of classical feminist concern' (A. Beezer, 104), remains ambivalent in its relationship with feminism. The titles *Cosmopolitan* gives to its features are ambiguous. *Cosmopolitan* does engage with a form of feminism, but the feminists it incorporates - Dale Spender, Erica Jong, Naomi Wolf - are distinctly of the Anglo-American school of feminism. Imagine *Cosmopolitan* including the vital, revolutionary feminism of the great trinity of French feminists, Luce Irigaray, Julia Kristeva and Hélène Cixous.

'Serious' articles are glamourized - with bold, colourful graphics, titles and photographs or illustrations. The *presentation* of *Cosmopolitan*, as with any magazine, brings everything onto the same level, visually, and semantically. This is called 'house style', but it also means that articles on serious issues such as domestic violence or abortion are given the same treatment, visually, as pieces about black shoes or types of lipstick.

The concept of 'femininity' in *Cosmopolitan*, however, is not static. The articles, after all, promote the notion of *change* as central to the concept of female identity promulgated by/ in the magazine. Change one's lover, one's friends, one's furniture, one's clothes, one's lifestyle. *Cosmopolitan* presents the idea of 'woman' or 'femininity' in flux. Magazines such as *Jackie, Just Seventeen, Mizz* and other teenage magazines are limiting, some critics claim. Angela McRobbie said that *Jackie* 'imprisons' its readers in notions of jealousy and competitiveness, in its portrayal of, for example, sexual relationships in the photostrips and stories. For McRobbie, *Jackie*

99 Janice Winship: "A Woman's World: *Woman* - an ideology of femininity", in CCCS, 1978

was a 'monolithic system', structured around a system of connoting codes: 'of romance, of personal life, of fashion and beauty, and of pop' (in A. Beezer, 109). McRobbie saw a single message emerging from *Jackie* and teen magazines, of consumerism, of cultural capitalism, whereas the teenage magazines were not reducible to a single reading/ meaning. According to McRobbie, through teenage magazines 'teenage girls are subjected to an explicit attempt to win consent to the dominant order – in terms of femininity, leisure and consumption, i.e., at the level of culture.'[100] Angela McRobbie's reading of *Jackie* and teenage magazines is too limiting; she makes, as so many critics do, simplistic assumptions about how and why people consume the products. This is the age-old problem for cultural studies, in particular post-semiological/ Marxism critical approaches, this link between text and reader, how much the text 'affects' or 'influences' the audience. This is where generalizations and assumptions come into play, where the critic says photostrips about love 'make it impossible for any girl to talk to, or think about a boy in terms other than those of romance' (McRobbie, 20) Here McRobbie goes too far, making a sweeping generalization which may be true in part, or for some of the time, but not for everyone.

  (Heterosexual) romance is still an abiding theme or desire in the world of magazines (and Western society in general). The notion of being together romantically (which equals sexually in the parlance of cynics and anthropologists) is still central. One sees this intense desire for companionship (and sex) in the lonely hearts classifieds and dating agency adverts. Some magazines (such as *Time Out*) have a thriving lonely hearts section, and the ads have become a staple ingredient of many newspapers. In every lonely hearts ad there is a mini-portrait and a mini-story waiting to be discovered, sometimes written in secret code, sometimes in abbreviations (GSOH for 'good sense of humour') and sometimes blatantly:

TALL, SENSUAL POST-GRAD, 27, tied, seeks tied but smouldering older woman to buy me lunch and ravage me thoroughly on occasional days of stringless escape; London; photo? Box No. AA 99
(*The Guardian*, 8 January, 1994)

100 A. McRobbie: *"Jackie*: An Ideology of Adolescent Femininity", 7

BI-GIRL, 28, sexy, slim and fit, wants naughty bi-female to burn off calories with. Must be fun and feminine. No man-haters please! Photo/ discretion vital. Box 425. (*Time Out*, 2 June, 1993)

•

CALIFORNIA BEACH BOY, 26, student, cute, with suntan, cosmopolitan, 6', gsoh, gch, etc. Seeks excellent babe. Any race/ nationality. No gays, no fat chicks!! Box 493
(*Time Out*, 13 October, 1993)

•

TRANSSEXUAL, 28, seeks handsome, hirsute man for romance. Photo ensures reply. Box 1698
(*Time Out*, 9-16 November, 1994)

•

SID THE SEXIST (41), caring, sensitive, romantic (and a big knob) seeks fat slag for the donation of a portion. Box 15886
(*Time Out*, 9-16 November, 1994)

•

Beki Dakin, Derbyshire: 'Darren, Wakefield. Remember warehouse '92-'93? I want to fuck your brains out. Please get in touch. I'm moving in September.'
(*Mixmag*, October, 1994)

There is a proto-feminist advert in the usually staid, domesticated *Woman's Journal* for Joseph Janard clothes. It is a role reversal scenario, where women do jobs traditionally associated with men. In this ad, we see a female artist, clutching paintbrushes, in an artist's studio. On a couch is a nude man. Instead of a male artist/ female model, we have female artist/ male model. But, as with a group of women enjoying a male stripper (another common gender role reversal), all is not quite so cut and dry. For example, the nude male model has a leaf over his genitals, while female artists' models are usually totally nude. Further, the man is in a half-reclining traditional nude pose but he holds his arms up, to flex his biceps. The male model is not allowed to be totally passive – he exhibits 'male' notions of strength with his flexed arm. And, though Joseph Janard's clothes are 'fashion for women who decide for themselves', this is a stereotypical photograph. The woman, for instance, is dressed in fashionable clothes: she is not a scruffy, bohemian painter, but a trendy, well-dressed model. The viewer may perhaps realize that the 'painter' in the end is in fact a fashion model. The photograph offers conflicting views

89

of femininity and masculinity, of passivity and activity, for the female painter is in fact a model. She's in the photograph precisely as a model, there in order to sell clothes.[101] There is another version of the Joseph Janard 'fashion for women who decide for themselves' ads which shows a woman in a suit, leaning over a table, talking forcefully to a group of businessmen. Here's the woman as high-powered business executive, dominant, assertive.[102]

In the world of magazines, any magazines, there is always an emphasis on the *next* thing, the *next* issue, the *next* product, the *next* event. It is the next relationship that will be The One; the next purchase from the High Street store that will really satisfy. Always there is an emphasis on the *new* and the *next*. On the future. On something happening around the corner. The media is built on desire and a search. A search for what, exactly? No one is quite sure of that. But viewers of MTV are encouraged to watch *just one more video*, magazine consumers are encouraged to buy the all-new fun-packed September issue. The multitudes of media products can only survive if people desire to buy them, if there is a desire for the *next* issue, the *next* show, the *next* download. Product proliferation only works if there is a huge appetite for more and more of what is essentially the same thing. The 'same but different'. The phrase, 'the same but different', describes accurately most (all?) media products, whether they are radio, television, newspapers, ads, 'women's magazines' or DVDs. The 'same but different', just dressed up differently.

Magazines blatantly repeat the same material in a variety of ways, just like all the media. Once they've found a winning formula, a successful mix of advertizing and editorial, they simply churn out variations on the tried and tested formula. Each issue of the same magazine tells the reader more of what s/he already knows. The content does vary, of course, but never very much. Readers (or any media consumers) are seen as being very conservative, so media producers change formats and content gingerly. Magazine production follows a simple formula, defined by Brian Braithwaite and Joan Barrell thus:

101 *Woman's Journal*, October 1994, 6-7
102 *Marie Claire*, October 1994, 126-7

> The magazine has to deliver what the reader wants and expects. If it does not, there is always another magazine which produces the formula a reader likes. (139)

There are many instances in 'women's magazines', in TV and radio ads, in all sections of the media, of feminist themes being subverted by 'femininity'. Notions of a feminist 'new woman' are taken so far then dropped in favour of a return to the values and attitudes of traditional (i.e., patriarchal) notions of 'femininity'. For example, the high-powered career-oriented woman, a media stereotype that emerged in the 1970s and 1980s, turns out often really to be hankering after her home and family and 'housewifely' duties. The socio-economically successful woman is shown, paradoxically, also as an object of desire. The successful (business) woman is fetishized by patriarchal culture, and is encouraged to fetishize herself. TV ads show women in powerful socio-economic roles then undermine them (by continually drawing attention to their appearance, for example) because they are threatening.

Cosmopolitan, She, InStyle, Allure, Marie Claire and other 'women's magazines' which claim to propound some form of feminism somewhere in their glossy pages, so often pull back and revert to traditional (patriarchal) economies. The 'go for it' mentality, the feminist 'you can do anything' dictum, which the upscale 'women's magazines' propound, is, at the last minute, ditched in favour of traditional, masculinist ethics. 'Women's magazines' cannot, finally, overthrow the patriarchal-consumerist order of things, because that would overturn the very world in which the magazines thrive. 'Women's magazines', like all magazines, like all media, need a patriarchal capitalist-consumerist culture in which to survive. They cannot seriously explore other socio-economic systems because they would alienate the very establishments on which they rely (advertizers and audiences).

If you look at the history of art, you see patriarchy at work in all depictions of women, from the nameless figurines of prehistoric Goddesses with their huge hips and buttocks, the so-called 'Stone Venuses', through the 'high art' nudes of Titian, Tintoretto, Rembrandt van Rijn and Peter

Rubens, to the photographs of Hollywood stars and contemporary mass pornography. *Cosmopolitan* and most 'women's magazines', then, simply promulgate this patriarchal view of women, where images and representations of women are constructed by masculinist ideologies. Although the staff of many 'women's magazines' are women, although the images in these magazines are female, although the discussions and features, the topics raised and the themes may be about women, still the overall slant is towards patriarchal representations of women.

Cosmetic surgery, then, can be seen as an attempt to counter the superficial masculinist views of what 'beauty' is in patriarchal society. Carrying the classified ads for cosmetic surgery, *Cosmopolitan* tacitly endorses it, just as the tabloid newspapers tacitly endorse pornography by publishing the soft porn telephone lines or websites. The very word 'cosmetic' implies a superficial, trivial, visual alteration of one's body. Cosmetic surgery may be simply the extension into flesh of other forms of body decoration. From eye-liner to tattoo to nose job. Whether we're talking about the forms of 'beauty' in non-Western societies in Papua New Guinea or Africa, or the 'high fashion' types on the streets of Manhattan or Milan, these views of 'beauty' are imposed by society, by a negotiation between the individual and society. The sadness of plastic surgery and liposuction is that people who have it done regard their appearance as so important. It's awful that people are seemingly made to feel self-conscious about the size of their breasts, for example. It's sad that people not only have hang-ups or neuroses about the size of their feet or hips or ears, they now have them cut and re-shaped. On the other hand, why not? In the late capitalist system, you can buy anything, including a new body. (And anything is for sale).

When *Cosmopolitan*, full of second wave feminist self-righteousness, printed the 'first full frontal male nude' in the 1970s (figures such as Burt Reynolds) it found out that the results were disappointing. It was not the revolution in publishing and feminism anticipated. 'For the fact is that is,' writes Richard Dyer, 'that the penis isn't a patch on the phallus. The penis can never live up to the mystique of the phallus.'[103] On the porn issue, it is worth remembering that many feminists are not bothered by it. According to writers such as Alison King, Avedon Carol and Christobel Mackenzie, porn sidetracks feminists from more pressing issues, such as race or poverty; pornography too often gets conflated with violence and sexism; 'pornography is just about men and women enjoying sex together', writes Avedon Carol, so what's the problem?; working in the porn industry may be 'demeaning', but isn't cleaning toilets or working in a factory also humiliating?; posing for photos may be less degrading than labouring for forty hours a week; many women like sex, and like to see and read about it; porn may not be more violent than other mainstream media – horror novels, for example, or Hollywood movies.[104] Pop star Madonna said a similar thing on US TV, pointing out that it was OK to have prime-time shows with violence and death, but not sex.

Cosmopolitan and the mainstream 'women's magazines' have an ambiguous attitude to pornography for the simple reason that most of them use sex to sell their magazines, just as advertizers use sex to sell products. Near-pornographic images can be found in nearly all 'women's magazines', of whatever kind. Some of these images would be censored even a few years ago. In the fashion glossies, such as *Vogue*, there has been a tradition of using erotic imagery, especially when produced by 'auteur' or 'art' photographers, the kind of high class 'erotic' photography of David Bailey, Helmut Newton, Bob Carlos Clarke *et al*. The 'high art' label helps imagery of sexual violence pass the censors – in TV advertizing as well as in mainstream magazines. The expensive sets, costumes, cars, jewellery, props, the slick production and sports cars enable the photos of bondage, S/M and fetishism to be viewed as 'fine art'. The porn debate is simply a sexier topic for mainstream magazines than issues such as childcare, inequality at work, racial discrimination or housework.[105]

When it comes to the so-called 'new women's porn', in magazines made

---

103 Richard Dyer: "Don't Look Now", *Screen*, 23, 3/4, 1983
104 See essays by Christobel MacKenzie, Alison King, Claudia, Avedon Carol and Feminists Against Censorship in Carol, 1993; also Chester, 1988
105 Gayle Rubin: "Misguided, dangerous and Wrong: An Analysis of Anti-Pornography Politics", in Carol, 1993, 38

largely by women for women (though many gay/ straight/ whatever men consume them too), *Cosmopolitan* and other 'women's magazines' are ambivalent about the 'new women's porn', for although *Cosmopolitan* has a 'positive' attitude to sex, and runs article after article on achieving multiple, cosmic orgasms, it does not 'officially' promote pornography. That might alienate consumers. The 'new women's porn' magazines fight the British censors: the typical example cited in the press is the battle to have the male erection shown. It's ironic that *Cosmopolitan* had been over this territory in the Seventies, and had abandoned male nudes. The 'new women's porn' magazines, however, happily deliver erotic fantasy material to women readers. This material was available earlier anyway - in 'shopping 'n' fucking' fiction (*Lace*, Jackie Collins, novels bought at airports), and in men's pornography. Some of the mainstream 'women's magazines' have taken up the 'new women's porn' - *Marie Claire* offered a free book of soft porn.

What *Cosmopolitan, InStyle, Marie Claire, Woman's Own, Best* and *More* steer well clear of, though, is the more 'extreme' or 'unusual' pornography; lesbian porn, *On Our Backs,* S/M porn, fetish porn, hardcore porn, and so on. Not for mainstream 'women's magazines' accounts of fistfucking, fucking with dildoes, female ejaculation, golden showers, dressing up in nappies, S/M bondage and the like.

Similarly, 'women's magazines' do not approach radical theory, whether lesbian, bi, queer or gay. Lesbian porn and radical lesbian and queer theory, for example, offers some challenging explorations of 'fucking with gender', but the mainstream 'women's magazines' have not found a way of incorporating it, and they would not wish to. It would be OK to have an article in the simultaneously 'serious'/ 'journalistic' and titillating/ entertaining format of *Marie Claire* o r *Cosmopolitan* on, say, cross-dressing or dildo sex, but not to incorporate radical lesbian or queer theory as part of the magazine's general credo.

All magazines create their own idea of their audience. Whoever their audience may actually be, each magazine has ideas, often conflicting, of just what that audience consists of. The *Cosmopolitan* audience is youngish (18-35, say), and not yet a mother. Articles on motherhood are left out and sexuality is highlighted. Indeed, one of the main criticisms levelled at *Cosmopolitan* is that it emphasizes sexuality too much. From the front page onwards, *Cosmopolitan* has many articles on sexuality, and has always done so. In the pre-AIDS era, *Cosmopolitan* exalted the empowered, sexual woman, self-confident, in control of her life and her sexuality. In the AIDS era, *Cosmopolitan* has simply altered its pieces on contraception to make 'safe sex' prominent. In the June 1994 issue of *Cosmo*, though, true 'safe sex' is not wearing a condom, but having no sex at all. Because sex, says *Cosmopolitan*, can hurt, emotionally. Sex is 'high-risk', writes Elsie Forster, 'because you could be disappointed, humiliated or physically hurt.'[106]

Cosmopolitan emphasizes heterosexuality. Strange that, for a magazine that claims to be 'feminist', and aimed at self-confident, career-minded women, lesbianism hardly features at all. While many lesbians are powerful, highly individual people who have made distinct choices about their sexuality, just the sort of person *Cosmopolitan* might profile, they hardly appear at all. All the mainstream 'women's magazines', from the 'traditional' *Woman/ Woman's Realm/ Me* type through the new low-priced weeklies, *Best* and *Bella*, to the 'glossy' magazines, *Vogue, Tatler* and *She,* assume a heterosexual, domesticated sort of sexuality.

'Women's greatest power is sexual', proclaims *Cosmopolitan* on its cover. Sadly, this kind of claim over-emphasizes sexuality at the expense of many other forms of power. For Andrea Dworkin, women don't have 'power' precisely because their sexuality is dominated by men, and taken from them. In Dworkin's simplistic power politics, men have the means to power, not women; men dictate the limits and methodologies of the social system, not women; men, not women, are dominant, sexually. Rape proves it, says Dworkin, as do violence, and pornography, etc.

The sexual politics of *Cosmopolitan* is essentially that of a watered-down Anglo-American feminism. *Cosmopolitan*'s feminism comes out of 'second-wave' 1970s feminism, the era of Gloria Steinem, Nancy Friday, Susan

106 Elsie Forster: "The Safest Sex of All", *Cosmopolitan*, June 1994, 131

Griffin, Robin Morgan, Kate Millett, Mary Daly and Andrea Dworkin. *Cosmopolitan*, like most if not all 'women's magazines', has embraced second wave Anglo-American feminism as the norm, but has hardly cast a glance at French feminism, for instance, at the work of Julia Kristeva, Monique Wittig, Luce Irigaray, Hélène Cixous, Xaviere Gauthier, etc. And as for acknowledging cultural theory and non-humanist feminism, forget it.

Cosmopolitan, like all 'women's magazines' except the most scholarly and erudite of tiny print-run magazines and journals, professes a feminism bound up in humanism. There is no kind of cultural criticism beyond the most simplistic being promulgated in 'women's magazines'. You're more likely to find progressive, radical feminism in the more traditionally masculinist genres such as film criticism (as in *Screen*, for instance). 'Shopping 'n' fucking' novels, the 'blockbusters' or 'bonkbusters', are the literary equivalent of *Cosmo*, but they do not, for example, offer radical revisions of female sexuality; a typical blockbuster, Shirley Conran's *Lace*, has orgasm described as '[s]oft, intense waves', exactly as in D.H. Lawrence's *Lady Chatterley's Lover*.[107]

Maybe it's too much to expect *Cosmopolitan* to deliver hard-hitting, polemical feminism. But certain aspects of the magazine, as with *Elle, Marie Claire* and *She*, hint at polemical feminism, a feminism which is challenging. Instead, we get articles on 'why men are so turned on by women's bottoms', and glib statements such as: 'women's greatest power is sexual'. The emphasis on sexuality in *Cosmopolitan*, as in *Marie Claire, Me, Bella* and *Prima*, always conforms to a received, establishment notion of women as 'objects', to be looked at lustfully by men. So, on the cover of *Cosmo*, we have 'what we love about men's bodies', and 'why oh why are terrorists so ugly?' (just kidding). As if sexual desire can be treated in three or four pages of a magazine article.

All right, let's look at the *Cosmo* article: why *are* men so desirous of 'women's bottoms'? Well, it turns out, the article tells us, that 'bottom fanciers' (here assumed to be male) 'aren't always obsessed with sheer size;

---

107 Shirley Conran: *Lace*, Penguin, 1982, 513; Avis Lewallen: "*Lace*: Pornography for Women?", in L. Gamman, 92

they also look for shape, proportion, movement – the whole works'.[108] The feature prints a selection of small photos of women, most semi-nude: Cher and her stage costume showing off her buttocks; Marilyn Monroe and Jane Russell in sparkly costumes; a woman in Lycra shorts, and so on. The photographs might appear in a soft porn magazine, in a 'nostalgia' spot: *Asses We Have Loved*, perhaps. Soft porn magazines often run features on, say, butts, or blowjobs, in exactly the same way that a photography magazine might print a survey of telephoto lenses.

In *Cosmopolitan*, the implication of the article is that you've got to get your ass in shape if you want to be loved. The writer, Lynn Snowden, is told to keep her bottom trim, so she does lunges and squats. Here, the connections between male desire and women being on show, between the images of women and their sexuality, is not at all questioned. Rather, it is couched in a mock serious tone, which hardly makes a dent on the vast realm of women's sexuality. All we get from this article is a few photos of buttocks and a female journalist telling us about being pinched on the bum at various times. There's no feminism here, instead, there's a weedy attempt at exploring sexuality, at how men look at women. This is typical of so many of the articles in the 'feminist' mainstream 'women's magazines': *Elle, Marie Claire, She, New Woman, Cosmopolitan*.

A series of three articles in the June, 1994 *Cosmopolitan* is entitled *Women On Top*, a familiar phrase from 1980s feminism. 'Cosmo celebrates women and power', runs the headline. 'Power feels great: so why don't women want it? It tastes good, feels good, let's you do good, and women who have it love it.'[109] Thus far, this series of articles sounds like powerful feminist empowerment. Ros Miles' feature makes some of the usual points, made a billion times in 'women's magazines', of the aphrodisiac quality of 'power' (power is sexy, etc), and cites various powerful people, or people who've grasped their own sense of power: John F. Kennedy, Hilary Clinton, Richard Branson, Amelia Earhart (the aviator), Anita Roddick, Margaret Thatcher, Eve Pollard, etc.

So far so good. The next article in the *Women On Top* series looks at

108 Lynn Snowden: "Who's a cheeky girl, then?" *Cosmopolitan*, June 1994, 166
109 Ros Miles: "Power Feels Great", *Cosmopolitan*, June 1994, 90

"The use and abuse of your sexual power".[110] Things go badly wrong for the *Cosmopolitan* article when Isobel Morgan asserts: 'You have sexual power when you make love on top' (p.106). No, not at all.

Making love on top does not 'give' you sexual power.

'Causing an erection' does not give you sexual power.

'Knowing how to flirt' does not give you sexual power.

Here, the *Cosmopolitan* pseudo-feminist stance becomes unstuck, because it is founded on an essentialist, biologist feminism, which French feminists such as Julia Kristeva and Monique Wittig have shown to be full of contradictions. *Cosmopolitan*, like all 'women's magazines', essentializes women, reduces them to a set of simplistic signs and values.

The over-dependence of *Cosmopolitan* on sexual politics is only one aspect of its ruthless stereotyping of women. While feminists such as Luce Irigaray state that '[t]he whole of my body is sexuate' (L. Irigaray, 1993, 53), critics of Irigaray's view of women's eroticism as two lips continually embracing say:

> All that 'is' woman comes to [Irigaray] in the last instances from her anatomical sex, which touches itself all the time. Poor woman.[111]

Sexuality is not just a matter of genitals rubbing together, or of making love on top, or of any number of biologist and essentialist issues. It is also shaped by notions of race, class, economy, status, politics, ideology and power. *Cosmopolitan* and other 'women's magazines' have to simplify their arguments, to squeeze information into three or four pages. But in doing so, they reduce feminism to a pitiful mouthing of platitudes. The emphasis on just one form of female sexuality (heterosexuality in almost all 'women's magazines') is a distinctly reductive and inauthentic kind of

---

110 Isbobel Morgan: "The use and abuse of your sexual power", *Cosmopolitan*, June 1994, 96-103
111 Monique Plaza: ""Phallomorphic power" and the psychology of "woman"", *Ideology and Consciousness*, 4, Autumn 1978, 32

feminism. [112]

An ad for Courvoisier cognac ('le cognac de Napoleon') shows a youngish white middle-class couple shot in soft focus in a restaurant, with a bowl of chocolates before them.[113] They are sitting drinking brandy after the candle-lit meal, shortly before leaping into bed. A Lady Jayne fashions advert shows a woman and a man about to kiss, in colour and close-up, over two pages. The copy to this heterosexual, romantic ad is:

> One look, THE look, and you know you're in for an enchanted evening. It starts with beautiful hair, irresistibly dressed with fashion accessories by Lady Jayne. It ends with a kiss... Or perhaps rather more?[114]

The 'rather more' here means a relationship, romance and, ultimately, tupping, of course. In other words, with the help of Lady Jayne hair fashions one might end up fucking someone at the end of the evening. A night which begins with 'beautiful hair' might end with 'rather more', i.e., 'heterosexual intercourse'. Throughout 'women's magazines' (all magazines, all media), we see these bourgeois romantic scenarios at work, where, at the end of the evening, fucking is the apotheosis, the 'happy ever after' ending of fairy tales, the delicious icing on the cake, the ultimate way of 'rounding off' a night out. It's a yawn, but Cinderella myths sell products. The romantic union of two (white, First World, middle-class) lovers sells watches: the Fil sports watch ad features two luscious nude people, suitably tanned and bereft of skin blemishes, entwined, eyes closed, caught in mid-fuck, so to speak.

The codes, morality, ideology and practices of 19th century fairy tales crop up everywhere, and especially in popular magazines and 'women's magazines' and also in 'romance' novels, movies, TV mini-series, soaps, TV news and so on. Look at soaps or Hollywood films: you find the stock

---

112 'If we define female subjectivity through universal biological/ libidinal givens, what happens to the project of changing the world in feminist directions? Further, is women's sexuality so monolithic that shared, typical femininity does justice to it? ... How can one libidinal voice – or the two vulval lips so startlingly presented by Irigaray – speak for all women?' Ann Rosalind Jones: "Writing the Body", in Showalter, 1986, 369

113 Courvoisier advert, *Woman's Journal*, January 1984, 22

114 Lady Jayne ad, *Clothes Show* magazine, December 1992

characters of fairy tales in stories shorn of their mythic power and degenerated to melodrama and soft porn: the jealous older woman, the novice who knows nothing as yet of sexuality or jobs ('just you wait!'), the ineffective, absent father, the recently married couple experiencing the first attacks of adultery and bitterness. In pulp romances, sit-coms and radio serials and *Vogue, Cosmo, Elle, Women's Realm, Bella*, the hells and ecstasies of fairy tales are ever present. The same punishments and laws abide in fairy tales and pulp romance fiction: be rebellious or disobey and pay for it; step outside societal norms and be punished or outcast; accept your due; work hard and you'll be rewarded; stick to good Christian morals; don't touch taboos; be kind to your parents; don't go through the graveyard/ forest/ city at night; bourgeois, romantic heterosexual marriage is expected of you, so wait wait wait, because 'someday your prince will come'.

One of the very few images of homosexuality in populist/ mainstream advertizing is the Benetton advert featuring two thirty-something white middle-class men with their arms around each other, smiling at the viewer. The colours of this ad connote stereotypical representations of gay maleness: one man wears a bright green shirt, the other a purply pink shirt. The copy is simply 'united colours of Benetton'.

In a piece on pornography in the popular weekly *Woman*,[115] a woman classed as 'The Model' (i.e., someone who works in the pornography industry as a 'model') says: 'I'm not being exploited, I'm exploiting men.' 'The newsagent', Brenda Appleby, 'owner of Candy Cards newsagent in Bognor Regis', states:

> I don't mind women showing their boobs. You can see that every day in *The Sun*. If women want to get paid for showing their body, well good luck to them, But I don't like it when they open up their legs - some of those photos are rather disgusting. (op.cit., 40)

Woman's Own was also following a second wave anti-porn feminist line in the 1980s: 'STOP THE TRADE IN FILTH - NOW' *Woman's Own* proclaimed in

---

115 Victoria Freedman: "Porn: Degrading? Harmless? Evil?", *Woman*, 9 March 1992, 40-41

1983.[116] In the homely monthly *Prima*, one of the success stories of British publishing, Laurie Graham writes of television's portrayal of sex and domesticates it:

> ...on television, while the camera lingers over the grunting and groaning, the plot stops and you are left wondering if you've go to time to water your fuchsias. It's all so unnecessary.[117]

In *Elle* (September, 1994) there is an article called "Women Who Buy Sex By the Hour", about women who pay men money to have sex. This is a kind of proto-feminism, where the tables are turned on men, so men are seen doing the roles and jobs of women. It is a rare kind of role-reversal, however. 'Women's magazines' have to really scrape around to find this kind of role-reversal story. In *Elle* there is an article on "Men on the game".[118] The piece looks at four men who are 'escorts', companions to women. The men charge about £30 ($45) an hour for being a companion. Sex is extra – between £100-£250 ($160-400). Sex is not discussed during the evening. At the end of the evening, however, says 'Mark', 'most women just come out and say, "How much for sex?"' (Weese, op.cit., 77) Here, men are portrayed as something women desire. As men say of women who dress in mini-skirts and stockings ('she's asking for it'), the article on male escorts or prostitutes presents women as really like men. At the end of the evening, women want sex, like men. The article panders to masculinist notions of sexual relations. The article says, well, women are like men really. They want sex too. If a man went out for an evening with a female escort, it would be assumed that readers would want to know if sex was discussed, desired, or latent under the surface in some way.

One of the most blatant displays of the nude body in the mainstream media is the cartoon strip "George and Lynne" that appears in Britain's most popular tabloid newspaper, *The Sun*. Unlike strips such as "Andy Capp" with its depiction of an argumentative working-class middle-aged

---

116 Angela Neustatter: "Stop the Trade in Filth – Now", *Woman' Own*, 14 May 1983
117 Laurie Graham, *Prima*, November 1993, 58
118 Sandra Weese: "Men on the game", *Elle*, September, 1994, 75-80

couple from 'oop North', in the tradition of *Coronation Street*, and unlike "Jane" or "The Gambols", "George and Lynne" are depicted in various states of undress.[119] His body as well as hers is depicted: sex has either just taken place, or, more frequently, it is about to take place. When their spirits are flagging, George and Lynne joke with each other, teasing each other about the lovemaking to come later. When things are bad, George can always watch Lynne's ass as she bends over looking for something or other. Her breasts continually spill out of her dressing gown. The couple are shown watching TV in the semi-nude, or sunbathing, or lounging around a swimming pool.

The article "50 things you should know about men"[120] in *Cosmo* is full of idiot generalizations, some jokey: '[m]en never go shopping unless they need something'. Many suggestions are plain stupid:

Men who write love letters don't live in this century.
Even men who consider themselves brave wouldn't want to be in the same room as Madonna.
Men always think that they're the best thing that's ever happened to you.

To show how stupid these assertions are, simply change the gender:

Women who write love letters don't live in this century.
Even women who consider themselves brave wouldn't want to be in the same room as Madonna.
Women always think that they're the best thing that's ever happened to you.

The cod feminism of *Cosmopolitan*, and *Marie Claire, Elle, Vogue, Bella, Best*, etc, has so many flaws and wrong assumptions it's difficult to know where to begin. For instance, in the June, 1994 *Women On Top* feature from *Cosmopolitan*, in the article on 'your sexual power', we find a table of 'Winners' and 'Losers', rather like those lists at the end of the year magazines of all kinds publish, showing what was 'in' and what was

119 Mike Featherstone & Mike Hepworth: "The Midlifestyle of "George and Lynne": Notes on a Popular Strip", in Featherstone *et al*, 1987; G. Perry & A. Aldridge: *The Penguin Book of Comics*, Penguin 1971
120 Rita Rudner, *Cosmopolitan*, October 1994, 49-51

'out' during the year. You might find 'blue' is 'out' and 'red' is 'in'. Or 'shades' are 'out' and 'contact lenses' are 'in'. Magazines are that banal, producing sad little lists of consumer or fashion items each year. In the *Cosmo* article, though, we find who *Cosmopolitan* regards as 'Winners' and 'Losers' in the realm of sexual power:

Winners	Losers
Joan Collins	Linda Lovelace
Brigitte Bardot	Marilyn Monroe
Princess of Wales	Duchess of York
Iman	Angie Bowie

These names require some explanation. In the media landscape, Joan Collins is a 'winner' because she has emerged as a high camp celebrity, a modern version of the ancient holy whore, a glam queen even at 60 years-old, star of glossy American soaps. Linda Lovelace, who was throat raped and abused, is a 'Loser'. Despite achieving media notoriety via the movie *Deep Throat*, Linda Marchiano/ Lovelace was seduced into prostitution and pornography, writes Andrea Dworkin. Marchiano 'was beaten on an almost daily basis, humiliated, threatened, including with guns, kept captive and sleep-deprived'.[121] *Cosmopolitan* readers are perhaps not aware of some of the darker, more sinister connotations of the name Linda Lovelace. Dworkin's information on Lovelace offers a picture of male brutality of extreme ruthlessness. The banality of the *Cosmopolitan* article is further heightened by pitting Lovelace as a 'loser' against the extremely lightweight, artistically/ culturally, Joan Collins, here called a 'winner'. For, as Dworkin says, Lovelace's escape from 'sexual slavery and her subsequent life as a mother, school teacher, and antipornography activist is a triumph of the human spirit – part of an unambiguous discourse of triumph.' (Dworkin, ib, 344) Joan Collins, meanwhile, has virtually nothing to say about anything.

The other 'Winners' and 'Losers' in the *Cosmo* article are similarly vapid: Iman is a 'Winner', while Angie Bowie ain't, because Iman married David

---

121 Dworkin: *Mercy*, 344; see Linda Lovelace & Mike McGrady: *Ordeal*, Citadel Press, 1980, and *Out of Bondage*, Lyle Stuart 1986

Bowie and Angie Bowie lost him. Oh dear. Marilyn Monroe is a 'Loser' because she suicided, while Brigitte Bardot became an activist, and renounced conventional notions of 'female beauty', the opposite of Joan Collins, who clings onto the idea of looking like a woman forty years her junior. Both faces, of Bardot and Collins, are patriarchally defined. Finally, the Princes of Wales is a 'Winner' in the *Cosmo* stakes, because she crusaded in the mid-1990s around the globe for causes while still remaining humble and beautiful, while the Duchess of York just exposes her breasts, sucks toes, and talks idiotically.

The banalities of *Cosmopolitan* and all the other 'women's magazines', this feminism dressed up in brilliantly coloured graphics, accompanied by photos of movie stars, and made into entertainment by a series of elisions and patronizing, glib statements, destroys the feminist cause/ crusade. When the writer says 'sexual power is yours, to do with as you will' (Morgan, op.cit., 97), it sounds great, it sounds like positive feminism. But it's not true. Power, sexual or otherwise, is not yours or anybody's, it is a social, political, psychological, ideological relation between people, between people and social systems, between people, systems, values, attitudes, cultures, etc. It's not something you can 'own', as you can 'own' a ladies' razor for shaving your legs.

If *Cosmopolitan*'s feminism seems to be a mess, some of the other 'women's magazines' are far, far worse. Few things are more depressing (but why?) in the media than magazine products, in print or TV, aimed at women. *Best* in 1994 includes features on diets, armchairs, TV dating shows, clinical depression, domestic violence, cakes, waist-coats, and kitchens (*Best*, 7 April, 1994). The following week's edition of *Best* features pieces on diets, pets, supermodels, nail-care, breast cancer, varicose veins, food allergies, dining rooms, baby switching, crockery sets, low paid workers, "Is it love...or just plain lust?", and so on. On one page of *Best* you find a piece on the romance of the Queen and Prince Philip, on the next page, how to cure headaches; on the next page, how to give up faking orgasms.[122] An article on 'single women' asks 'why do women have

---

122 *Best*, 13 August 1992, 41, 43, 45

such a tough time being alone?'[123] In *Me*, in 1994, we find the usual celebrity snaps, organ donation, HIV screening, hysterectomy, bed linen, saving tigers, "The Big Five Sex Myths", skin care, marriage counselling, tables, back pain, and spiritual healing. In *New Woman*, we are told about 'cosmic orgasms', complete with swirling stars, flying, flashing lights and music.[124] 'Women's magazines' cheerfully appropriate the fantastic and escapist, as well as the mundane and the everyday.

Although the internet has been yet another element that has helped to drive down sales of magazines (and newspapers) in the 2000s and 2010s, 'women's magazines' continue to thrive. And will likely do so for some time – or at least, the issues, the celebrity-based stories, the health and beauty pages, and the repetitive emphasis on heterosexual romance and sex will doubtless carry on in some form or another.

123 Rebecca Rice: "Single wise women", *Cosmopolitan*, May 1994, 140
124 Jane Alexander: "Psychedelic Sex", *New Woman*, August 1994, 64-65

BIBLIOGRAPHY

All books are published in London, England, unless otherwise stated

Connie Alderson: *Magazines Teenagers Read*, Pergmanon, 1986

Alison Assiter & Avedon Carol, eds: *Bad Girls and Dirty Pictures: The Challenge to Reclaim Feminism*, Pluto Press, 1993

Anne Beezer *et al*: "Methods For Cultural Studies Students", in D. Punter, ed. *Introduction to Contemporary Cultural Studies*, Longman, London, 1986, 95-118

Frances Bonner *et al*, eds: *Imagining Women Cultural Representations and Gender*, Polity Press, Cambridge, 1992

Rachel Bowlby: *Just Looking: Consumer Culture in Dreiser, Gissing and Zola*, Methuen, 1985

—"Modes of Modern Shopping: Mallarmé at the *Bon Marché*", in N. Armstrong, 1987

—*Still Crazy After All These Years*, Routledge, 1992

R. Braidotti: *Patterns of Dissonance: A Study of Contemporary Philosophy*, Polity Press, 1991

Brian Braithwaite & Joan Barrell: *The Business of Women's Magazines*, Kogan Page, 1988

Judith Butler: *Gender Trouble: Feminism and the Subversion of Identity*, Routledge, 1990

—& J.W. Scott, eds: *Feminists Theorise the Political*, Routledge, 1992

Claudia Card, ed: *Adventures in Lesbian Philosophy*, Indiana University Press, 1994

CCCS Women's Studies Group: *Women Take Issue*, Hutchinson, 1978

Gail Chester & Julienne Dickey, ed: *Feminism and Censorship: The Current Debate*, Prism Press, Bridport, Dorset, 1988

Hélène Cixous: *A Hélène Cixous Reader*, ed. Susan Sellers, Routledge, 1994

Eric Clark: *The Want Makers*, Hodder & Stoughton, 1988
Nancy Cott: *The Grounding of Modern Feminism*, Yale University Press, New Haven, 1987
Rosalind Coward: *Female Desire: Women's Sexuality Today*, Paladin, 1984
Alice Courtney & Thomas Whipple: *Sex Stereotyping in Advertising*, Lexington Books, Lexington, 1983
Mary Daly: *Pure Lust: Elemental Feminist Philosophy*, Women's Press, 1984
Robert D'Amico: "Desire and the commodity form", *Telos*, 35, 1978
Irene Dancyger: *A World of Women*, Gill & Macmillan, Dublin, 1978
H. Davis & P. Walton, eds: *Language, Image, Media*, Blackwell, 1983
G. Day & C. Bloch, eds: *Perspectives on Pornography: Sexuality in Film and Literature*, Macmillan, 1988
—*Readings in Popular Culture: Trivial Pursuits?*, Macmillan, 1990
Laura Doan, ed: *The Lesbian Postmodern*, Columbia University Press, New York, 1994
Andrea Dworkin: *Intercourse*, Arrow, 1988
—*Pornography: Men Possessing Women*, Women's Press, 1984
—and Catherine MacKinnon: *Pornography and Civil Rights: A New Day for Women's Equality*, Organizing Against Pornography, Minneapolis, 1988
Gillian Dyer: *Advertising as Communication*, Methuen, 1982
Richard Dyer: *Stars*, British Film Institute, 1979
—*Only Entertainment*, Routledge, 1992
Ira Ellenthal: "*Vogue*: 'the ultimate authority'", *Product Marketing*, March, 1979
J. Epstein & K. Straub, eds: *Body Guards: The Cultural Politics of Gender Ambiguity*, Routledge, New York, 1991
Frank Farmer: "The effect of colour supplements on women's magazines", *Admap*, August, 1981
Mike Featherstone: "The body in consumer culture", *Theory, Culture & Society*, 1, 2, 1983
—*et al*, eds: *The Body*, London, 1989
Marjorie Ferguson: *Forever Feminine*, Heinemann, 1983
—"Imagery and ideology: the cover photographs of traditional women's magazines", in Tuchman, 1978
S. Franklin *et al*, eds: *Off Centre: Feminism and Cultural Studies*, HarperCollins, New York, 1992
Jane Gallop: *Thinking Through the Body*, Columbia University Press, New York, 1988
—*Feminism and Psychoanalysis: the daughter's seduction*, Macmillan, 1982
Lorraine Gamman & Margaret Marshment, eds: *The Female Gaze: Women as Viewers of Popular Culture*, Women's Press, 1988
Pamela Church Gibson & Roma Gibson, ed: *Dirty Looks: Women, Pornography, Power*, British Film Institute, 1993

C. Gledhill, ed: *Stardom: Industry of Desire*, Routledge, 1991

Erving Goffmann: *Gender Advertisements*, Macmillan, 1979

Robert Goldman: *Reading Ads Socially*, Routledge, 1992

Gabriele Griffin *et al*, eds: *Stirring It: Challenges For Feminism*, Taylor & Francis, 1994

Susan Griffin: *Pornography and Silence: Culture's Revenge Against Nature*, Women's Press, 1981

Elizabeth Grosz: *Sexual Subversions*, Allen & Unwin, 1989

Mary Beth Haralovitch: "Advertising Heterosexuality", *Screen*, 23, no. 2, 1982

Anne Hollander: *Seeing Through Clothes,* Viking Press, New York, 1980

Patricia Hollander: "The page three girl speaks to women, too", *Screen*, 24, 3, 1983

Lucy Hughes-Hallett: "The cosy secret of a jolly good Reed", *The Standard*, 8 February, 1982

Maggie Humm: *Feminisms: A Reader*, Harvester Wheatsheaf, 1992

—ed: *The Dictionary of Feminist Theory*, Harvester Wheatsheaf, 1989

—*Feminist Criticism: Women as Contemporary Critics*, Harvester, 1986

Luce Irigaray: *Je, tu, nous: Toward a Culture of Difference*, tr Alison Martin, Routledge, 1993

—*Thinking the Difference: For a Peaceful Revolution*, Athlone Press, 1994

—*The Irigaray Reader,* ed Margaret Whitford, Blackwell, Oxford, 1991

Mary Jacobus, ed: *Women Writing and Writing About Women*, Croom Helm, 1979

Sut Jhally: *The Codes of Advertising: Fetishism and the Political Economy of Meaning in the Consumer Society,* Routledge, New York, 1990

—"Probing the Blindspot: The Audience Commodity", *Canadian Journal of Political and Social Theory*, vol. 6, no 1-2, 1982

S. Kappeler: *The Pornography of Representation*, Polity Press, Cambridge, 1986

Ann Karpf: "Do the glossies gloss over feminism?", *New Statesman*, 1 November, 1985

Julia Kristeva: *The Kristeva Reader*, ed Toril Moi, Blackwell, 1986

—*Desire in Language: A Semiotic Approach to Literature and Art*, ed Leon Roudiez, tr Thomas Gora, Alice Jardine & Leon Roudiez, Blackwell, 1982

—*About Chinese Women*, tr A. Barrows, Boyars, 1977

Annette Kuhn: *The Power of the Image: Essays on Representation and Sexuality*, Routledge, 1985

Jacques Lacan and the *Ecole Freudienne: Feminine Sexuality,* ed. Juliet Mitchell and Jacqueline Rose, Macmillan, 1982

Robin Lakoff & Raquel Scherr: *Face Value: The Politics of Beauty*, Routledge, Boston, 1984

Elaine Marks & Isabelle de Courtivron, eds: *New French Feminisms: an Anthology*, Harvester Wheatsheaf, 1981

Angela McRobbie, ed: *Zoot Suits and Second-Hand Dresses: An Anthology of Fashion and Music,* Macmillan, 1989

—*Postmodernism and Popular Culture,* Routledge, 1994

—& M. Nava, eds: *Gender and Generation,* Macmillan, 1984

—*Feminism and Youth Culture: From Jackie to Just Seventeen,* Macmillan, 1991

—*"Jackie*: An Ideology of Adolescent Femininity", Centre for Contemporary Cultural Studies, 53, 1978

—& Trish MacCabe, eds: *Feminism For Girls,* Routledge, 1981

Kate Millet: *Sexual Politics,* Doubleday, New York, 1970

Trevor Millum: *Images of Woman: Advertising in Women's Magazines,* Chatto, 1975

Toril Moi: *Sexual/ Textual Politics: Feminist Literary Theory,* Methuen, 1985

Moira Monteith, ed: *Women's Writing: A Challenge to Theory,* Harvester Press, Brighton, Sussex, 1986

Laura Mulvey: *Visual and Other Pleasures,* Macmillan, 1989

Sally Munt, ed: *New Lesbian Criticism: Literary and Cultural Readings,* Harvester Wheatsheaf, 1992

Greg Myers: *Words in Ads,* Edward Arnold, 1994

Kathy Myers: *Understains: The Sense and Seduction of Advertising,* Comedia, 1986

—"Fashion 'n' Passion", *Screen,* 23, 3/4, 1982

Lynda Nead: *Female Nude: Art, Obscenity and Sexuality,* Routledge, 1992

Linda Nicholson, ed: *Feminism/ Postmodernism,* Routledge, 1990

Onlywomen, ed: *Love Your Enemy? The Debate Between Heterosexual Feminism and Political Lesbianism,* Onlywomen Press, 1981

H.L. Radtke & H.J. Stam, eds: *Gender and Power,* Sage, 1994

Janice Radway: *Reading the Romance: Feminism and the Representation of Women in Popular Culture,* University of North Carolina Press, Chapel Hill, 1984

Rayna Rapp: "Is the legacy of second wave feminism postfeminism", *Socialist Review,* January/ March, 98, 1988

J.L. Reich: "Genderfuck: The Law of the Dildo", *Discourse: Journal of Theoretical Studies in Media and Culture,* vol. 15, no. 1, 1992, 112-127

Patrice Retro: "Mass Culture and the Feminine", *Cinema Journal,* 25, 1986, 5-21

Philip Rice & Patricia Waugh, eds: *Modern Literary Theory: A Reader,* Arnold, 1992

Adrienne Rich: *Blood, Bread and Poetry,* Virago, 1980

John Sanders: "Teen magazines: reflection of the frightening eighties", *Campaign,* 25 February, 1983

Sue Sarsby: *Romantic Love and Society,* Penguin, 1983

C. Schwichenberg: *The Madonna Connection: Representational Politics, Subcultural Identities and Cultural Theory,* Westview Press, Boulder, CO, 193

Sue Sharpe: *Just Like a Girl,* Penguin, 1976

Elaine Showalter, ed: *The New Feminist Criticism,* Virago, 1986

Dale Spender: *The Writing or the Sex? why you don't have to read women's writing to know it's no good*, Pergamon Press, New York, 1989

Susan Rubin Suleiman, ed: *The Female Body in Western Culture: Contemporary Perspectives*, Harvard University Press, Cambridge, Mass., 1986

Alan Tomlinson, ed: *Consumption, Identity and Style*, Routledge, 1990

Gay Tuchman *et al*, eds: *Hearth and Home*, Oxford University Press, 1978

Barry Turner, ed: *The Writer's Handbook, 1993,* Macmillan, 1992

Cynthia White: *Women's Magazines 1693-1968*, Michael Joseph, 1970

Margaret Whitford: *Luce Irigaray: Philosophy in the Feminine*, Routledge, 1991

S. Wilkinson & C. Kitzinger, eds: *Heterosexuality: A Feminism and Psychology Reader*, Sage, 1993

Linda Ruth Williams: *Critical Desire: Psychoanalysis and the Literary Subject*, Arnold, 1995

Judith Williamson: *Consuming Passion: The Dynamics of Popular Culture*, Marion Boyars, 1986

—*Decoding Advertisements*, Marion Boyars, 1978

Janice Winship: *Inside Women's Magazines*, Pandora, 1987

—"Woman becomes an "individual" - femininity and consumption in women's magazines, 1954-1969", CCCS, University of Birmingham, 1981

—"Femininity and women's magazines", Unit 6, *U221, The Changing Experience of Women*, Open University, 1983

—""Options - for the way you want to live now", or a magazine for superwoman", *Theory, Culture & Society*, 1, 3, 1983

—""A girl needs to get streetwise": magazines for the, 1980s", *Feminist Review*, 21, Winter, 1985

John W. Wright, ed: *The Commercial Connection*, Delta, New York, 1979

Writers' & Artists' Yearbook, 1989, A. & C. Black, 1989

Jack Zipes: *Don't Bet on the Prince: Contemporary Feminist Fairy Tales in North American and England*, Gower, 1986

Lisbet van Zoonen: *Feminist Media Studies*, Sage, 1994

ILLUSTRATIONS

• Examples of magazines covers of *Cosmopolitan* magazine.
(National Magazine Company).

• Covers of *She, Bliss, Mizz, Sugar, Jackie, FHM, GQ, Arena, Vogue, New Woman, Radio Times, Elle, Smash Hits, Just Seventeen, People, Woman, Woman's Own, Best, Company, Good Housekeeping, Marie Claire,* and *Glamour* magazines.
(National Magazine Company. IPC Media. Panini. EMAP. D.C. Thomson. Conde Nast. BBC Magazines. Hachette Filipacchi. EMAP Metro.)

• Advertizing from women's magazines.

• Samples pages from *Marie Claire.* (IPC Media).

Covers of Cosmopolitan magazine,
2008, above, 2007, below.

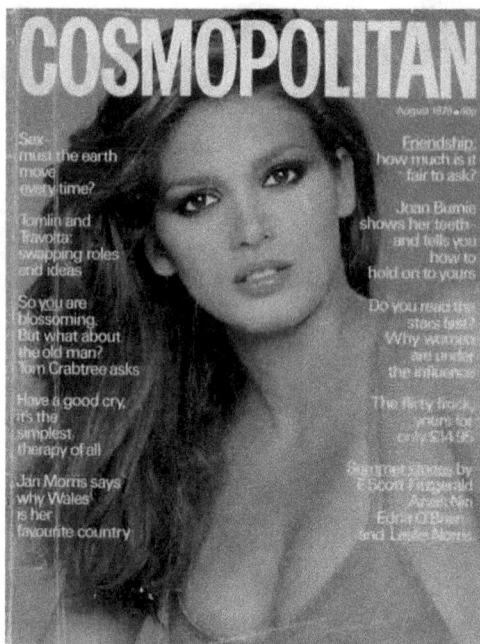

More examples of covers
from Cosmpolitan, including 1979, above.

Covers of Cosmopolitan (2004, left)

COSMOPOLITAN

THE #1 WOMEN'S MAGAZINE

Wake Up Gorgeous!

SEX SECRETS

AROUSE HIM LIKE CRAZY!

- 3 Surprising Pleasure Triggers
- How to Hit His G-Spot
- Where He Hopes You'll Linger

45 Ways to Get Even Closer to Him

Great Butt and Thighs

A Top Trainer's Best Advice

10 Subliminal Tricks That Make People Adore You

Katherine Heigl

THE MOST SATISFYING SEX POSITION

It Turns Him On... and It Feels Awesome for You

John Mayer Shares Why All Guys Aren't A**holes

PLUS:

cosmopolitan.com

COSMOPOLITAN

FASHION WEEK

BE A SEX GODDESS

Instant Glam GO FROM DRAB TO DIVA IN UNDER 10 MINUTES!

MILES TO GO BEFORE I WED

Toxic Friends

Sensational **Summer Fragrances**

Is your Christmas turkey safe to eat?

29 NOVEMBER 2005
ISSUE 48 70p

Bella

WHO TOOK HANNAH?
The mystery of my
missing daughter
is solved at last

PARTY BY POST
Affordable clothes
delivered to your door

BETRAYED!
The copper who
stole my wife

The tastie
Christmas trea
tried & tested for yo

Lose 5lb this week
3 new diets to
get slim *FAST*

LOST A STONE   I LOST 3st   I LOST 2st

CLASSROOM CUPID
My star pupil led me
to the man of my dreams

Top trees
at prices
you'll love

SPECIAL DOUBLE ISSUE

EXCLUSIVE
PHOTOS!

People

JENNIFER'S BIG DAY
Triathlon to Marc's
Surprise 40th Party

People
BEST
& WORST
DRESSED!
PLUS WORST HAIR. WHAT'S IN, WHAT'S OUT
AND HOW TO GET THE LOOK

AND
EVERYTHING
FABULOUS!

EVA LONGORIA
'I'm Just Fat'
–Not Pregnant

BRITNEY
Hosts an Emotional
Family Reunion

BAD HAIR DAYS   GOSSIP GIRL STYLE   CHIC AT ANY AGE

Bella, November, 2005, above.
People, September, 2004, left.

COMPANY magazine

www.getlippy.com
June 2008

ONLY £2

EXCLUSIVE
Rihanna
On bondage, British
men & being a diva!

50+
SUPER
SEXY
BIKINIS
from just £6

FOUND!
YOUR SECRET
sex
WEAPONS

9 770141 114232   06>

'Drugged while I went
out for a cigarette'
Company investigates
the new rape danger

Say 'NO'
to sunbeds
Which WAGs
stripped for
our campaign?

MIRACLES!
THE 30 BEST SERUMS, SHAMPOOS
& STRAIGHTENERS
AS VOTED BY YOU

Bungalow & Banksy,
back-combing
How 'Now' are you?

Bye-bye
PERIODS
The NEW contraception
that could change your life

Company magazine, June 2008

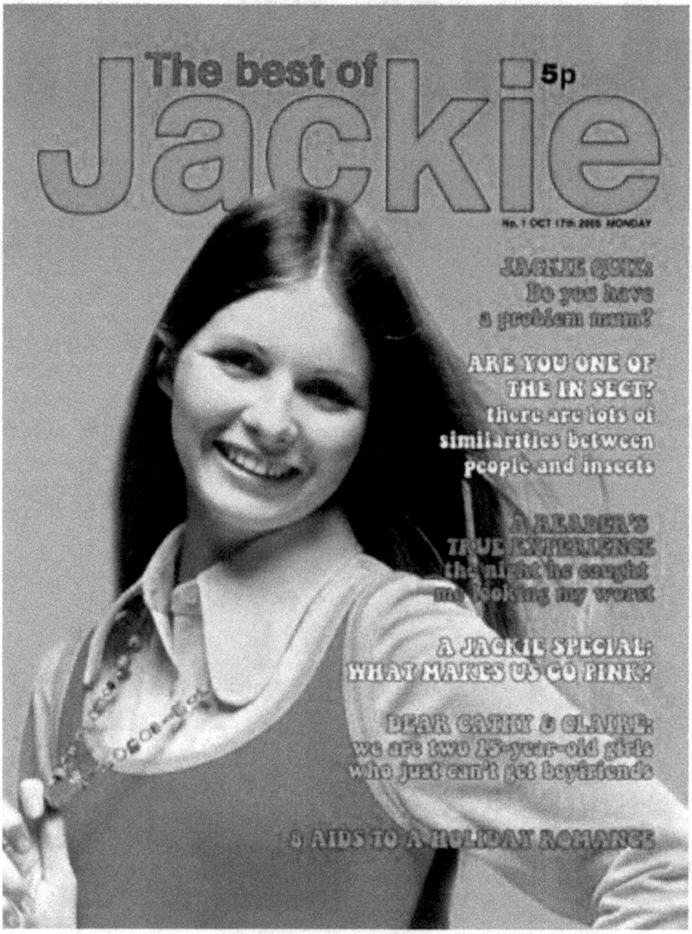

Jackie magazine

New Woman, below,
Marie Claire, above.
Both from 2008.

Sugar, 2007, above.
Vogue, below.

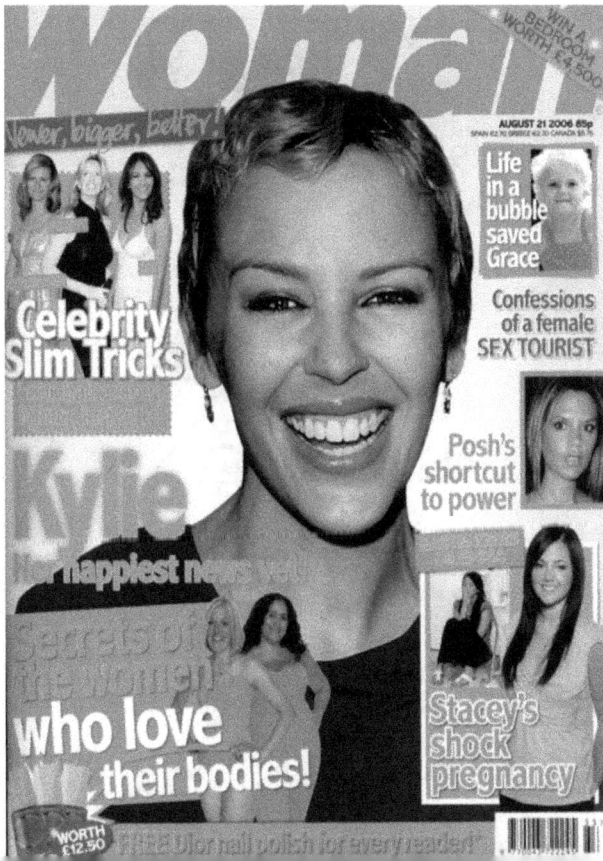

Woman's Own, 2005. above. Woman, 2006, below.

Bliss magazine

Elle magazines, 2007.

Just Seventeen, June, 1991

Mizz magazine,
Sept, 2006, below.
May, 2007, left.

Good Housekeeping, September, 2004, right.
Radio Times, February, 1996, below.

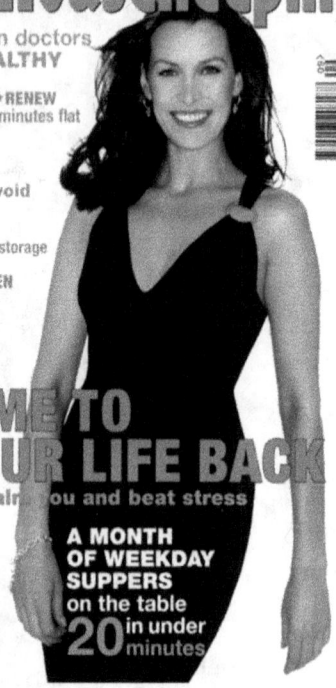

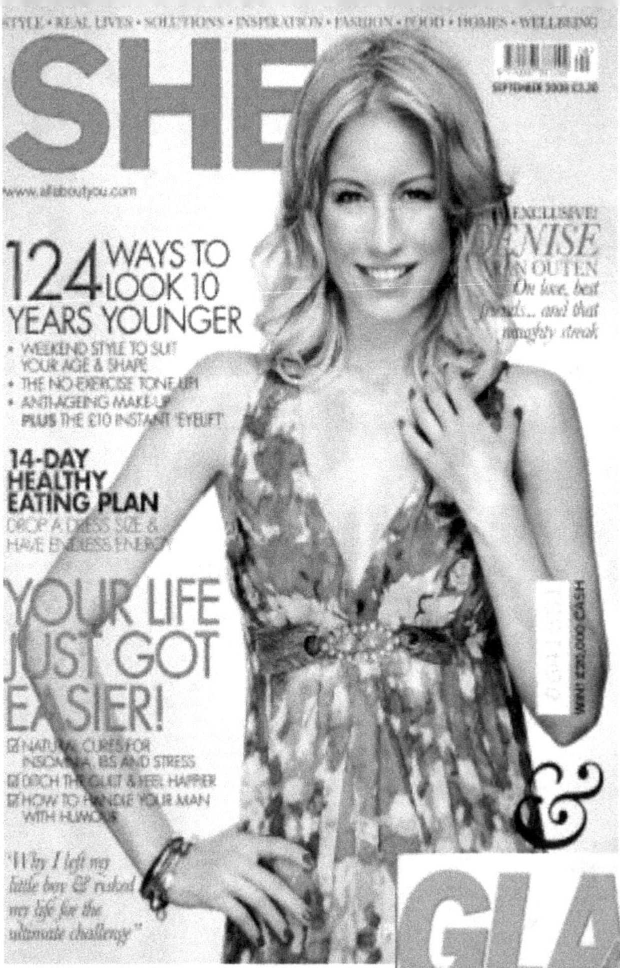

She magazine, 2008, left.
Glamour magazine, 2007, below.

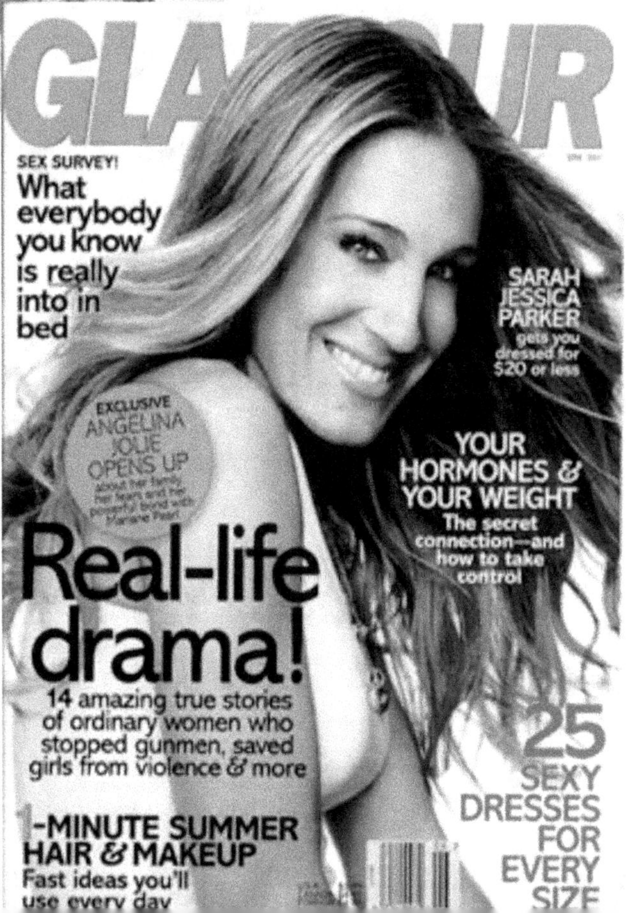

Registered by Australia Post — Publication No. NBQ 7796
$1.60 (New Zealand $2.20 incl GST) 24 August 1987

SMASH HITS

The Final Countdown In Color

Meet Billy Idol Competition

KYLIE MINOGUE

"Sometimes I don't want to be like this"

FREE GIANT POSTER INSIDE

Samantha Fox & Billy Idol

Boom Crash Opera

David Bowie

Party Boys

George Michael

A-ha

Pat Cash

Boy George

Madonna

Smash Hits, August, 1987

HELLO BOYS.

THE ONE AND ONLY
wonderbra

THE ORIGINAL PUSH-UP PLUNGE BRA AVAILABLE IN SIZES 32-38ABC

Bra wars

An ad for Wonderbra shows a woman (who is white, bourgeois, young)
wearing nothing but a bra, staring at the camera. She is model Eva
Herzigova, from the Czech Republic, who has a '36B superbosom'. In an
interview in Looks magazine, where Eva Herzigova is hilariously introduced
"Cup hands, here comes Eva…", the model says 'I'm happy to show them off
while they look pretty'.
The copy line is 'LOOK ME IN THE EYES AND TELL ME THAT YOU LOVE ME'.
An alternative is: 'HELLO, BOYS!' and 'AND GOD CREATED WOMAN (ALMOST)'.
In another Wonderbra ad, in Cosmopolitan, Eva Herzigova stands looking at the
viewer, topless except for the prominent bra. The copy line is 'MIND IF I BRING
A COUPLE OF FRIENDS?'. Another Wonderbra ad shows Eva Herzigova smiling
at the viewer, wearing a bra, her arms open to reveal her breasts. The opposite page
says 'NOTICE ANYTHING DIFFERENT ABOUT ME?'

The Bride wore Charnos

Examples of 'She woman', from She, April, 1994

ARENA

May 2007 £3.90

Photographed exclusively for ARENA by Perou

THE CONTROVERSY ISSUE

The UK's most notorious women

Starring

Lily Cole

The body of the year!

KATE MOSS, AMY WINEHOUSE, PEACHES GELDOF, ABIGAIL CLANCY

2 COLLECTORS' COVERS!

PLUS!
Lauren Laverne
Frank Miller
on Sin City 2
Mirko Cro Cop
Rob Brydon
+
Skinhead
scarves

PLUS!

Filthy Fiction!

Sex stories by Britain's hottest authors p152

PLUS! **HOW THE INTERNET IS DESTROYING EVERYTHING!**

+ ARENA BRINGS BACK NATIONAL SERVICE!

Men's style magazines:
Arena, 2007, above.
GQ, 2006, below.

'Lads' mags': FHM, October, 1995

FEBRUARY 2007 £2.90 UK EDITION

marie claire

NEW LO

www.marieclaire.co.uk

Catwalk can-do
Top trends to suit your style

New year, new career

SEIZE THE MOMENT AND CHANGE YOUR LIFE NOW

SAND
BULLO
EXCLUSI

Plu
SECRETS
THE COSMET
SURGEON
THE STA

WALL TO WALL VIPs! INSIDE THE MOST GLAM PARTIES EVER

EXTRA! EXTRA!

The SHOPS

THE BEST FOR HIGH STREET FASHION

Marie-Claire, UK edition, February, 2007.
Illustrations on this page and over are taken from this edition.

PREE
STEAL

RIVIERA
CHIC

e moneyed
our in
sticated
white
lue. By
ie Cooper.
ographs by
Militscher

L

RICE £282
c. £64.99
d; cotton vest,
nhams; denim
, Lee: leather
45, Russell &
See Directory
t details

COME CLOSER
MATTE PERFECTION
THIS AIR-SOFT
MUST BE TOUCHED

MEET
DREAM MATTE
MOUSSE
THE UK'S NO.1 FOUNDATION*

Our air-whipped mousse gives
you such pure matte perfection
with an amazing air-soft feel.
Blends so evenly, perfects
completely.

There's nothing else quite like
Dream Matte Mousse.
Feel the difference.

8 matte-perfecting shades.

MAYBELLINE
NEW YORK
MAYBE SHE'S BORN WITH IT. MAYBE IT'S MAYBELLINE

LANCÔME
PARIS

spree v steal

Make you and your bank manager happy with this relaxed weekend look. By Lucia Stasi

£110

£6

£99

Stainless steel watch
with leather strap, D&G Time

Stainless steel watch
with leather strap,
New Look

£12

Cotton shirt, A.P.C.

Cotton shirt,
Primark

£80

£25

£210

£49

Cashmere vest,
Crumpet

Silk/cashmere-mix
vest, Soft Grey at
La Redoute

Denim jeans,
Citizens of Humanity

Denim jeans,
Boden

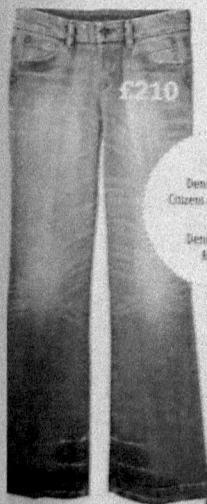
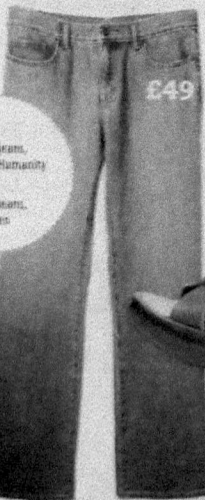

£340

Leather and wood
sandals, Chloé

Leather and wood
sandals, Faith

£75

www.realsimple.co.uk 55

THE ART OF
ANDY GOLDSWORTHY

COMPLETE WORKS: SPECIAL EDITION
(PAPERBACK and HARDBACK)

by William Malpas

A new, special edition of the study of the contemporary British sculptor,
Andy Goldsworthy, including a new introduction, new bibliography and many
new illustrations.

This is the most comprehensive, up-to-date, well-researched and in-depth
account of Goldsworthy's art available anywhere.

Andy Goldsworthy makes land art. His sculpture is a sensitive, intuitive
response to nature, light, time, growth, the seasons and the earth. Goldsworthy's environmental art is becoming ever more popular: 1993's art book
Stone was a bestseller; the press raved about Goldsworthy taking over a
number of London West End art galleries in 1994; during 1995 Goldsworthy
designed a set of Royal Mail stamps and had a show at the British Museum.
Malpas surveys all of Goldsworthy's art, and analyzes his relation with other
land artists such as Robert Smithson, Walter de Maria, Richard Long and
David Nash, and his place in the contemporary British art scene.

The Art of Andy Goldsworthy discusses all of Goldsworthy's important and
recent exhibitions and books, including the *Sheepfolds* project; the TV docu-
mentaries; *Wood* (1996); the New York Holocaust memorial (2003); and
Goldsworthy's collaboration on a dance performance.

Illustrations: 70 b/w, 1 colour. 330 pages. New, special, 2nd edition.
Publisher: Crescent Moon Publishing. Distributor: Gardners Books.

ISBN 1-86171-059-3 (9781861710598) (Paperback) £25.00 / $44.00

ISBN 1-86171-080-1 (9781861710802) (Hardback) £60.00 / $105.00

ANDY GOLDSWORTHY
IN CLOSE-UP

SPECIAL EDITION (HARDBACK and PAPERBACK)

by William Malpas

A new, special edition of our bestselling title, exploring Andy Goldsworthy's artworks in detail. A good, all-round introduction to Goldsworthy's art.

Illustrations: 160 b/w, 4 colour. 260 pages. Second edition. Hardback. Publisher: Crescent Moon Publishing. Distributor: Gardners Books.

ISBN 1-86171-094-1 (9781861710949) (Hbk) £60.00 / $105.00

ISBN 1-86171-091-7 (9781861710919) (Pbk) £25.00 / $44.00

Available from bookstores. amazon.com, play.com, tesco.com, and other web-sites.
In the United States from Baker & Taylor, (800) 7753760 or (800) 7751100
or (908) 5417062. electser@btol.com or btinfo@btol.com.

ANDY GOLDSWORTHY

TOUCHING NATURE:
SPECIAL EDITION

(PAPERBACK and HARDBACK)

by William Malpas

A new, special and updated edition of our bestselling title, providing
an excellent general introduction to the art of Andy Goldsworthy.

Illustrations: 75 b/w, 2 colour. 354 pages. Third edition. Paperback.

Publisher: Crescent Moon Publishing. Distributor: Gardners Books.

ISBN 1-86171-056-9 (9781861717) (Paperback) £25.00 / $44.00

ISBN 1-86171-087-9 (9781861710871) (Hardback) £60.00 / $105.00

THE ART OF
RICHARD LONG

COMPLETE WORKS : SPECIAL EDITION
(HARDBACK and PAPERBACK)

by William Malpas

A new study of the British artist Richard Long, an important contemporary international artist. The most detailed, in-depth exploration of Richard Long's art currently available.

Illustrations: 48 b/w, 2 colour. 439 pages.
First edition. Hardback and paperback editions.

Publisher: Crescent Moon Publishing. Distributor: Gardners Books.

ISBN 1-86171-079-8 (9781861710796) (Hardback) £60.00 / $105.00

ISBN 1-86171-081-X (9781861710819) (Paperback) £25.00 / $44.00

LAND ART

A COMPLETE GUIDE TO LANDSCAPE, ENVIRONMENTAL, EARTHWORKS, NATURE, SCULPTURE AND INSTALLATION ART

by William Malpas

A new, special edition of our popular book on land art.
Chapters on land artists such as Robert Smithson, Walter de Maria, Christo, Michael Heizer, Richard Long and Andy Goldsworthy.

Illustrations: 35 b/w, 2 colour. 314 pages. First edition. Paperback.

Publisher: Crescent Moon Publishing. Distributor: Gardners Books.

ISBN 1-86171-062-3 (9781861710628) £25.00 / $44.00

J.R.R. Tolkien
The Books, The Films, The Whole Cultural Phenomenon

by Jeremy Mark Robinson

A new critical study of J.R.R. Tolkien, creator of Middle-earth and author of *The Lord of the Rings, The Hobbit* and *The Silmarillion*, among other books.

This new critical study explores Tolkien's major writings (*The Lord of the Rings, The Hobbit, Beowulf: The Monster and the Critics, The Letters, The Silmarillion* and *The History of Middle-earth* volumes); Tolkien and fairy tales; the mythological, political and religious aspects of Tolkien's Middle-earth; the critics' response to Tolkien's fiction over the decades; the Tolkien industry (merchandizing, toys, role-playing games, posters, Tolkien societies, conferences and the like); Tolkien in visual and fantasy art; the cultural aspects of The Lord of the Rings (from the 1950s to the present); Tolkien's fiction's relationship with other fantasy fiction, such as C.S. Lewis and *Harry Potter*; and the TV, radio and film versions of Tolkien's books, including the 2001-03 Hollywood interpretations of *The Lord of the Rings*.

This new book draws on contemporary cultural theory and analysis and offers a sympathetic and illuminating (and sceptical) account of the Tolkien phenomenon. This book is designed to appeal to the general reader (and viewer) of Tolkien: it is written in a clear, jargon-free and easily-accessible style.

754pp   ISBN 1-86171-057-7   £25.00 / $37.50

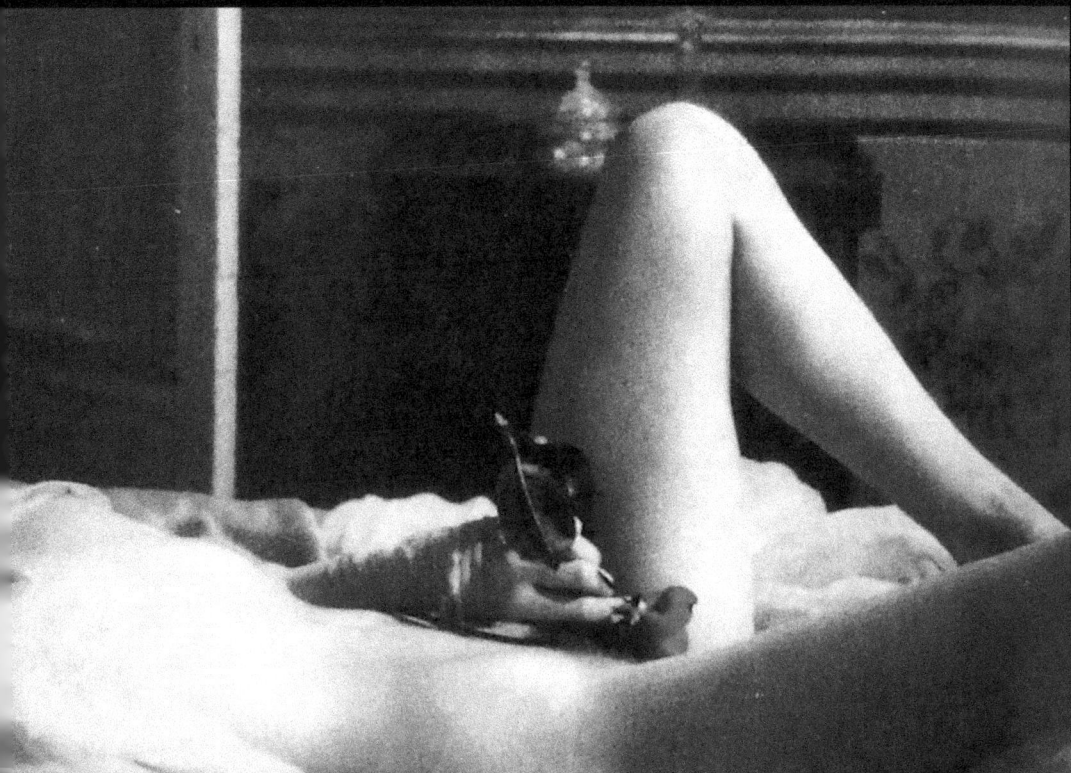

Walerian Borowczyk

Cinema of Erotic Dreams

by Jeremy Mark Robinson

Walerian Borowczyk (1923-2006) was a Polish artist, animator and filmmaker who lived in France for much of his life. He is the author of European art cinema masterpieces Goto: Island of Love, Blanche and Immoral Tales, some surreal animated shorts, and controversial films such as The Beast. This new book concentrates on Borowczyk's feature films, from Goto to Love Rites, which contain some of the most extraordinary images and scenes in recent cinema. Erotica for some, porn for others, Borowczyk's films are highly idiosyncratic and unforgettable.

Bibliography, notes, illustrations   240pp.
Paperback   ISBN 9781861712301   £15.00 / $30.00

Jean-Luc Godard

The Passion of Cinema /
Le Passion de Cinéma

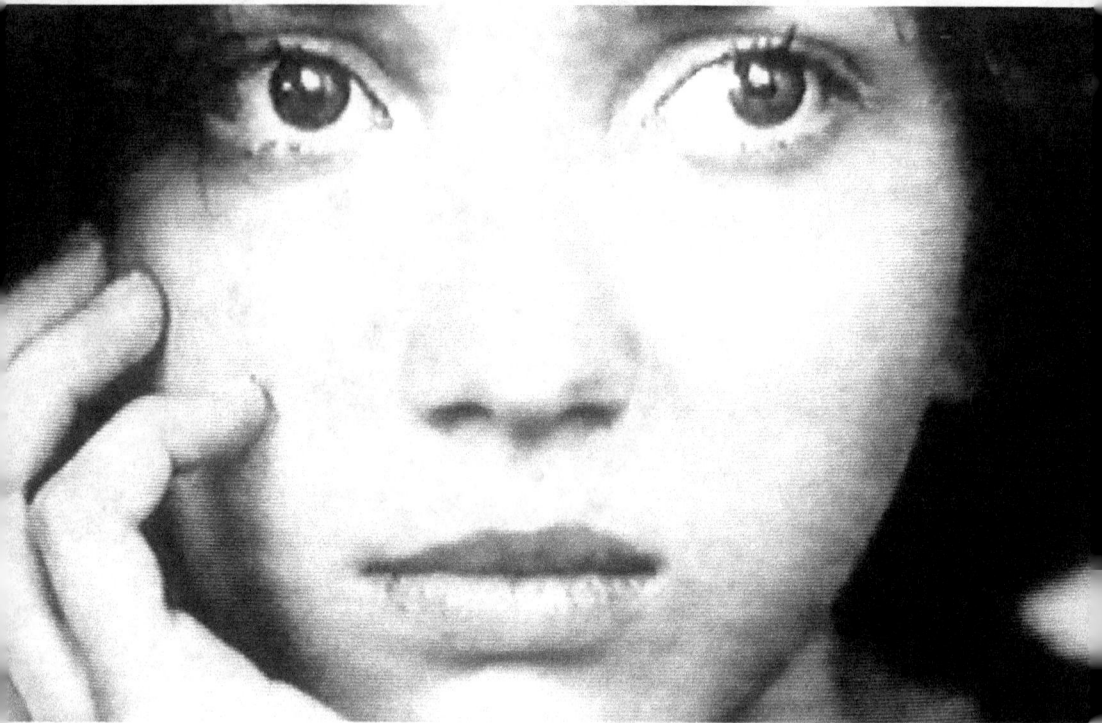

by Jeremy Mark Robinson

A new study of the French filmmaker Jean-Luc Godard (b. 1930), director of iconic films such as *Breathless, Weekend, Pierrot le Fou, Passion* and *Vivre Sa vie*. This book explores 27 of Godard's major films, from *Breathless* to *Notre Musique*, and includes a scene by scene analysis of Godard's controversial 1985 movie of the Virgin Mary, *Je Vous Salue, Marie*.

Bibliography, notes, illustrations   420pp
Hardback   ISBN 9781761712271   £50.00 / $100.00

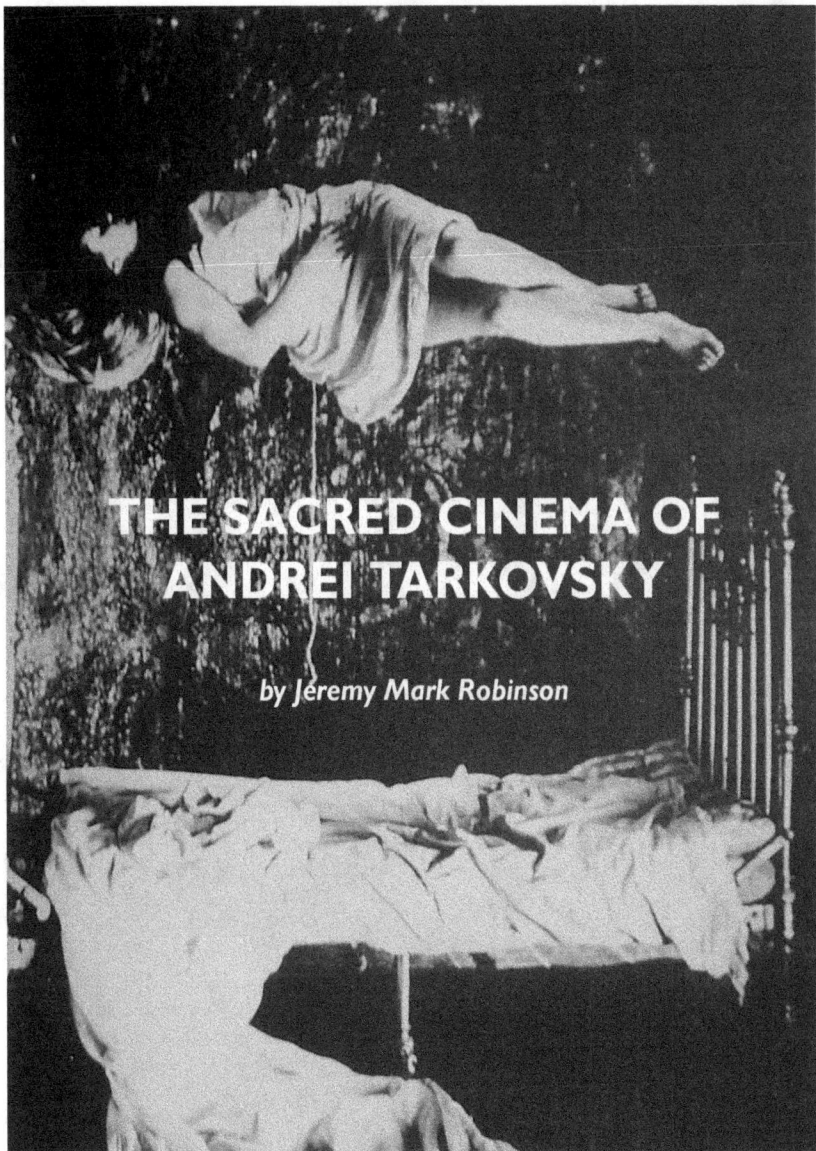

THE SACRED CINEMA OF ANDREI TARKOVSKY

by Jeremy Mark Robinson

A new study of the Russian filmmaker Andrei Tarkovsky (1932-1986), director of seven feature films, including *Andrei Roublyov, Mirror, Solaris, Stalker* and *The Sacrifice*.

This is one of the most comprehensive and detailed studies of Tarkovsky's cinema available. Every film is explored in depth, with scene-by-scene analyses. All aspects of Tarkovsky's output are critiqued, including editing, camera, staging, script, budget, collaborations, production, sound, music, performance and spirituality. Tarkovsky is placed with a European New Wave tradition of filmmaking, alongside directors like Ingmar Bergman, Carl Theodor Dreyer, Pier Paolo Pasolini and Robert Bresson.

An essential addition to film studies.

Illustrations: 150 b/w, 4 colour. 682 pages. First edition. Hardback.

Publisher: Crescent Moon Publishing. Distributor: Gardners Books.

ISBN 1-86171-096-8 (9781861710963) £60.00 / $105.00

Life, Life
Selected Poems

Arseny Tarkovsky

translated and edited by Virginia Rounding

Arseny Tarkovsky is the neglected Russian poet, father of the acclaimed film director
Andrei Tarkovsky. This new book gathers together many of Tarkovsky's most lyrical
and heartfelt poems, in Rounding's clear, new translations. Many of Tarkovsky's poems
appeared in his son's films, such as *Mirror, Stalker, Nostalghia and The Sacrifice*.
There is an introduction by Rounding, and a bibliography of both Arseny and Andrei Tarkovsky.

Bibliography and notes   110pp   2nd ed   ISBN 1-86171-114-X   £10.00 / $20.00

In the Dim Void

Samuel Beckett's Late Trilogy:
Company, Ill Seen, Ill Said and
Worstward Ho

by Gregory Johns

This book discusses the luminous beauty and dense, rigorous poetry of Beckett's late works, *Company, Ill Seen, Ill Said* and *Worstward Ho*. Johns looks back over Beckett's long writing career, charting the development from the *Molloy-Malone Dies-Unnamable* trilogy through the 'fizzles' of the 1960s to the elegiac lyricism of the *Company* series. Johns compares the trilogy with late plays such as *Ghosts, Footfalls* and *Rockaby*.

Bibliography, notes. 120pp
ISBN 1861710712 and ISBN 1861712356   £10.00 / $20.00

CRESCENT MOON PUBLISHING

ARTS, PAINTING, SCULPTURE

The Art of Andy Goldsworthy: Complete Works
Andy Goldsworthy: Touching Nature
Andy Goldsworthy in Close-Up
Andy Goldsworthy: Pocket Guide
Andy Goldsworthy In America
Land Art: A Complete Guide
Richard Long: The Art of Walking
The Art of Richard Long: Complete Works
Richard Long in Close-Up
Richard Long: Pocket Guide
Land Art In the UK
Land Art in Close-Up
Land Art In the U.S.A.
Land Art: Pocket Guide
Installation Art in Close-Up
Minimal Art and Artists In the 1960s and After
Colourfield Painting
Land Art DVD, TV documentary
Andy Goldsworthy DVD, TV documentary
The Erotic Object: Sexuality in Sculpture From Prehistory to the Present Day
Sex in Art: Pornography and Pleasure in Painting and Sculpture
Postwar Art
Sacred Gardens: The Garden in Myth, Religion and Art
Glorification: Religious Abstraction in Renaissance and 20th Century Art
Early Netherlandish Painting
Leonardo da Vinci
Piero della Francesca
Giovanni Bellini
Fra Angelico: Art and Religion in the Renaissance
Mark Rothko: The Art of Transcendence
Frank Stella: American Abstract Artist
Jasper Johns: Painting By Numbers
Brice Marden
Alison Wilding: The Embrace of Sculpture
Vincent van Gogh: Visionary Landscapes
Eric Gill: Nuptials of God
Constantin Brancusi: Sculpting the Essence of Things
Max Beckmann
Egon Schiele: Sex and Death In Purple Stockings
Delizioso Fotografico Fervore: Works In Process 1
Sacro Cuore: Works In Process 2
The Light Eternal: J.M.W. Turner
The Madonna Glorified: Karen Arthurs

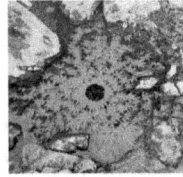

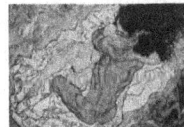

LITERATURE

J.R.R. Tolkien: The Books, The Films, The Whole Cultural Phenomenon
The *Earthsea* Books of Ursula Le Guin
Beauties, Beasts and Enchantment: Classic French Fairy Tales
Tolkien's Heroic Quest
Sexing Hardy: Thomas Hardy and Feminism
Thomas Hardy's *Tess of the d'Urbervilles*
Thomas Hardy's *Jude the Obscure*
Thomas Hardy: The Tragic Novels
Love and Tragedy: Thomas Hardy
The Poetry of Landscape in Hardy
Wessex Revisited: Thomas Hardy and John Cowper Powys
Wolfgang Iser: Essays
Petrarch, Dante and the Troubadours
Maurice Sendak and the Art of Children's Book Illustration
Andrea Dworkin
Cixous, Irigaray, Kristeva: The *Jouissance* of French Feminism
Julia Kristeva: Art, Love, Melancholy, Philosophy, Semiotics and Psychoanalysis
Hélene Cixous I Love You: The *Jouissance* of Writing
Luce Irigaray: Lips, Kissing, and the Politics of Sexual Difference
Peter Redgrove: Here Comes the Flood
Peter Redgrove: Sex-Magic-Poetry-Cornwall
Lawrence Durrell: Between Love and Death, East and West
Love, Culture & Poetry: Lawrence Durrell
Cavafy: Anatomy of a Soul
German Romantic Poetry: Goethe, Novalis, Heine, Hölderlin
Feminism and Shakespeare
Shakespeare: Love, Poetry & Magic
The Passion of D.H. Lawrence
D.H. Lawrence: Symbolic Landscapes
D.H. Lawrence: Infinite Sensual Violence
Rimbaud: Arthur Rimbaud and the Magic of Poetry
The Ecstasies of John Cowper Powys
Sensualism and Mythology: The Wessex Novels of John Cowper Powys
Amorous Life: John Cowper Powys and the Manifestation of Affectivity (H.W. Fawkner)
Postmodern Powys: New Essays on John Cowper Powys (Joe Boulter)
Rethinking Powys: Critical Essays on John Cowper Powys
Paul Bowles & Bernardo Bertolucci
Rainer Maria Rilke
Joseph Conrad: *Heart of Darkness*
In the Dim Void: Samuel Beckett
Samuel Beckett Goes into the Silence
André Gide: Fiction and Fervour
Jackie Collins and the Blockbuster Novel
Blinded By Her Light: The Love-Poetry of Robert Graves
The Passion of Colours: Travels In Mediterranean Lands
Poetic Forms

POETRY

Ursula Le Guin: Walking In Cornwall
The Best of Peter Redgrove's Poetry
Peter Redgrove: Here Comes The Flood
Peter Redgrove: Sex-Magic-Poetry-Cornwall
Dante: Selections From the Vita Nuova
Petrarch, Dante and the Troubadours
William Shakespeare: Sonnets
William Shakespeare: Complete Poems
Blinded By Her Light: The Love-Poetry of Robert Graves
Emily Dickinson: Selected Poems
Emily Brontë: Poems
Thomas Hardy: Selected Poems
Percy Bysshe Shelley: Poems
John Keats: Selected Poems
D.H. Lawrence: Selected Poems
Edmund Spenser: Poems
Edmund Spenser: Amoretti
John Donne: Poems
Henry Vaughan: Poems
Sir Thomas Wyatt: Poems
Robert Herrick: Selected Poems
Rilke: Space, Essence and Angels in the Poetry of Rainer Maria Rilke
Rainer Maria Rilke: Selected Poems
Friedrich Hölderlin: Selected Poems
Arseny Tarkovsky: Selected Poems
Arthur Rimbaud: Selected Poems
Arthur Rimbaud: A Season in Hell
Arthur Rimbaud and the Magic of Poetry
Novalis: Hymns To the Night
Paul Verlaine: Selected Poems
D.J. Enright: By-Blows
Jeremy Reed: Brigitte's Blue Heart
Jeremy Reed: Claudia Schiffer's Red Shoes
Gorgeous Little Orpheus
Radiance: New Poems
Crescent Moon Book of Nature Poetry
Crescent Moon Book of Love Poetry
Crescent Moon Book of Mystical Poetry
Crescent Moon Book of Elizabethan Love Poetry
Crescent Moon Book of Metaphysical Poetry
Crescent Moon Book of Romantic Poetry
Pagan America: New American Poetry

MEDIA, CINEMA, FEMINISM and CULTURAL STUDIES

J.R.R. Tolkien: The Books, The Films, The Whole Cultural Phenomenon
Cixous, Irigaray, Kristeva: The *Jouissance* of French Feminism
Julia Kristeva: Art, Love, Melancholy, Philosophy, Semiotics and Psychoanalysis
Luce Irigaray: Lips, Kissing, and the Politics of Sexual Difference
Hélène Cixous I Love You: The *Jouissance* of Writing
Andrea Dworkin
'Cosmo Woman': The World of Women's Magazines
Women in Pop Music
Discovering the Goddess (Geoffrey Ashe)
The Poetry of Cinema
The Sacred Cinema of Andrei Tarkovsky
Walerian Borowczyk: Cinema of Erotic Dreams
Jean-Luc Godard: The Passion of Cinema
John Hughes and Eighties Cinema
The Cinema of Richard Linklater
Liv Tyler: Star In Ascendance
The Cinema of Donald Cammell
The Cinema of Hayao Miyazaki
Blade Runner and the Films of Philip K. Dick
Paul Bowles and Bernardo Bertolucci
Media Hell: Radio, TV and the Press
An Open Letter to the BBC
Detonation Britain: Nuclear War in the UK
Feminism and Shakespeare
Wild Zones: Pornography, Art and Feminism
Sex in Art: Pornography and Pleasure in Painting and Sculpture
Sexing Hardy: Thomas Hardy and Feminism

In my view *The Light Eternal* is among the very best of all the material I read on Turner. (Douglas Graham, director of the Turner Museum, Denver, Colorado)

The Light Eternal is a model monograph, an exemplary job. The subject matter of the book is beautifully organised and dead on beam. (Lawrence Durrell)

It is amazing for me to see my work treated with such passion and respect. (Andrea Dworkin)

Sex-Magic-Poetry-Cornwall is a very rich essay... It is like a brightly-lighted box. (Peter Redgrove)

CRESCENT MOON PUBLISHING
P.O. Box 393, Maidstone, Kent, ME14 5XU, United Kingdom.
01622-729593 (UK) 01144-1622-729593 (US) 0044-1622-729593 (other territories)
cresmopub@yahoo.co.uk   www.crescentmoon.org.uk